It was Napoleon who said, "There is no place in a fanatic's head where reason can enter." He could well have been thinking of the militant deaf chauvinists who stop at nothing in their incomprehensible determination to keep deaf infants deaf, to prevent deaf children from learning English and becoming literate, to preserve and intensify the isolation and insularity of the deaf, to fight to the death against medical and technologic advances towards overcoming deafness and its pernicious effects.

Tom Bertling is the crusading knight who is challenging those fanatics, in defense of the coming generation of children who deserve a better fate than to be sacrificial pawns in a futile effort to preserve what those fanatics call "culture." If this be "genocide," make the most of it!

-Otto J. Menzel, Ph.D., Editor
LIFE AFTER DEAFNESS

Following the success of the autobiographical "A Child Sacrificed to the Deaf Culture," Tom Bertling's second book "No Dignity for Joshua" continues the revelation by a "Deaf of Deaf" insider from the Deaf community. His insights into the realities of the Deaf community, especially regarding sexual abuse of children, are disturbing and should lead to greater oversight of residential deaf schools. Bertling's writing skills evidence the advantage of early exposure to hearing and even a short period of mainstreamed oral education. Tom Bertling is the conscience of the Deaf-World.

> *-Thomas J. Balkany, MD, FACS, FAAP*
> *Hotchkiss Distinguished Professor and*
> *Vice Chairman, Dept. of Otolaryngology*
> ***UNIVERSITY OF MIAMI***

From the oppression of deaf children to the bashing of Miss America, Bertling dissects the inner-workings of a small but powerful group who wield tremendous influence over our nation's culturally-deaf community.

It is amazing to me how all this explosive material Bertling covers has missed the scrutiny of the mainstream press!

> *-Paula Bonillas, Editor and Publisher*
> ***HEARING HEALTH***

NO DIGNITY FOR JOSHUA

A famous saying goes... "The truth hurts." This will have special relevance for Deaf ASL militants. While they comprise only a small percentage of deaf people, they practically dominate deaf-related policies and language-related decisions both nationally and internationally.

The world needs more people like Tom Bertling to advocate on behalf of saving a crucial language for the deaf--ENGLISH.

This book "No Dignity for Joshua" speaks for itself.

-Frances M. Parsons
Retired Associate Professor and Author
GALLAUDET UNIVERSITY

Tom Bertling addresses language and cultural issues which have been mostly ignored (by culturally-deaf leaders) in this enlightening book which should have been written decades ago.

"No Dignity for Joshua" goes a long way in exposing long-standing abuses and cover-ups in the deaf community. I know of only a few deaf community leaders who are ready to accept responsibility "for their part in how things are." Hopefully now others will step forward and work for solutions.

-Terry Ryther, President
THE COMMUNITY EAR

NO DIGNITY FOR JOSHUA

TO THE READERS OF *NO DIGNITY FOR JOSHUA:*

This book is a reality check. The deaf community is hardly a utopia, having the same shortcomings as any other society, and it is only fair that readers have access to this information.

I have concerns for deaf education, for culturally-deaf leaders' motives, and for the need for social reforms in the deaf community, and I would like to see more culturally-deaf people achieve social responsibility for themselves.

Our society thrives on a system of checks and balances. If this book increases awareness of this subject in our society then it has served its purpose and will ultimately benefit the deaf community in the long run.

I'd like to thank Dr. Thomas Balkany, Prof. John Knutson, Joshua Ladd, Dr. Otto Menzel, Prof. Frances Parsons, Diane Prairie, Sam Sperline, and especially Valerie Jo and Rikki Sage.

Tom Bertling

KODIAK MEDIA GROUP
Publishers of vital educational and scholastic material.
Available domestically and worldwide through your bookstore and most major book wholesalers and distributors or you may contact the publisher directly. Large quantity educational discounts available.

4

NO DIGNITY FOR JOSHUA

*More vital insight into Deaf Children,
Deaf Education and Deaf Culture.*

TOM BERTLING

KODIAK MEDIA GROUP
Educational and Scholastic Publications

NO DIGNITY FOR JOSHUA

First edition published 1997

10 9 8 7 6 5 4 3 2 1

For further information contact: KODIAK MEDIA GROUP
                                     P.O. Box 1029-B2
                                     Wilsonville, Oregon 97070

SAN: 297.9993

ISBN: 0-9637813-6-7

U.S. Library of Congress Catalog Card Number: 96-78647

PUBLISHER'S CATALOGING IN PUBLICATION DATA:
Bertling, Tom
No Dignity for Joshua.
  Bibliography and index.
  1. Deafness-children. 2. Deaf culture. 3. Parents of handicapped/disabled children. 4. Deaf education-schools. I Title.

Kodiak Media Group is a privately-owned company and receives no private or public (including non-profit) special-interest funding or grants.
kjosh96/c/486

CONTENTS

NO DIGNITY FOR JOSHUA

*There is very little agreement among all the factions involved with the education of the deaf child. Parents of deaf children must explore all possibilities, then weigh all the advantages against the disadvantages to make the best decision for **their** child. Parents should also be wary of proponents of methods of educating the deaf that seem to be mostly criticism of other methods.*

Some of the names, places, titles, and genders may have been changed, deleted or fictionalized to protect the privacy of people involved. Experiences and examples I have cited may have been condensed and/or combined with others along with modifying sequences for a clear, coherent and to the point reading while preserving facts and truths.

*It is **not my intent to identify or ridicule** anyone personally in this book. Only individuals who have already publicly spoken out or have become part of the published public record may have been identified in the reference section.*

People foraying into deaf issues have wide and varied opinions on this subject matter. Readers taking note of quotes and references used in this book are urged to refer to these writers' actual material before drawing an absolute conclusion of the message they are conveying.

This author's views are based upon personal experiences and opinions and he does not pretend to be the final and absolute authority on this subject matter.

NO DIGNITY FOR JOSHUA

FOREWORD

Like my first book, "A Child Sacrificed to the Deaf Culture," this book was written especially for parents of deaf children, deaf educators and administrators, as well as those having a professional or social interest in the deaf.

To my regret I still cannot report on the deaf community in glowing terms. Efforts to improve the deaf community are being hampered by the actions of culturally-deaf *militants*. Problems of sexual abuse to deaf children are largely left to those outside the culturally-deaf community to resolve. Doctors face the wrath of the these leaders over every new medical advance on deafness. Efforts to get culturally-deaf leaders to co-exist with other deaf factions are simply rejected. Contradictions, lies and censorship from culturally-deaf leaders confuse and mislead many, both inside and outside the deaf community. The list goes on endlessly.

These dismal conditions have a direct negative impact on the majority of deaf people who are clearly not represented by these deaf militants and certain culturally-deaf leaders.

There is a huge misconception in our society. Many perceive the deaf community as a utopia, a safe haven for deaf children and adults. Nothing could be farther from the truth. Some members of the deaf community mistreat and abuse others in the community, often times very badly. The deaf

9

community is not isolated from the ills of our society. Criminal and moral problems infest the deaf world. Physical, and especially sexual abuse is prevalent and even tolerated. Suicide, alcoholism and drug abuse is common. Even the number of deaf people who have the HIV virus is considerable. The deaf community is very often a mirror of the mainstream society.

There are a number of deaf individuals who are working to resolve these problems. Unfortunately, others are pre-occupied with efforts to *preserve* a deaf culture. Utilizing extreme and radical behavior to attain their goals and attract media attention, these *militant* deaf leaders have convinced many they represent *all* deaf people.

The fact is, the majority of deaf people do not agree with these militants. While one can sympathize with their fears of historically being oppressed, many deaf leaders have simply gone overboard and have become consumed with power.

Today, deaf people find themselves at a historic crossroad. Technology opened a promising new avenue. Medical advances provided another. But culturally-deaf leaders seem to be herding us all down the path to oblivion.

CHAPTER ONE
NO DIGNITY FOR JOSHUA

At a state residential school for the deaf, Joshua was kneeling in the hall outside the dorm director's office with his face inches from the wall. While most of the other young deaf children were outside enjoying extracurricular activities in the afternoon before dinner, Joshua knelt for hours nearly every day in his private hell, wondering when Mrs. Multnomah, a dorm staff member, would come out and slap the back of his head again.

Joshua (not his real name) was being punished, not for misbehaving or a misdeed, but simply for having an additional disability besides being deaf. He was a convenient scapegoat for all the problems on Mrs. Multnomah's ward. Joshua simply did not measure up to her standard for a deaf child. Because of his other physical problems, which among other things necessitated the use of leg braces, Joshua was deliberately kept away from the other deaf kids by Mrs. Multnomah. He was not "pure" enough in her irrational and prejudicial way of thinking.

As the months went by, most of the other deaf children and many of the dorm staff members came to believe he deserved this endless disciplining and *expected* to find him kneeling in the hall. The mistruths became normalized.

11

NO DIGNITY FOR JOSHUA

Today however, Joshua was burdened with additional worries. Last night he was raped again by several older students. Since his leg braces were removed nightly, rendering him nearly helpless to escape, he simply endured. He could not see the perpetrators. But he had a pretty good idea who they were as their smirks could be spotted across the institutional grounds. Besides, whom was he going to tell? Who would believe Joshua, the erroneously designated troublemaker? The last time he told his family, they called Mrs. Multnomah, who in turn assured them this did not happen. Afterwards, Mrs. Multnomah dished out additional punishments. Joshua wasn't going to repeat *that* cycle again.

When Joshua's hearing loss was discovered as an infant, his family was burdened with a father in the state prison. While his mother deeply cared for him, she was overwhelmed personally and had to struggle to provide for herself, Joshua and two other siblings.

As a result of this, when Joshua reached school age, he had very little language formation and communicational skills. Doctors and public school officials suggested sending him to a residential deaf school. As the easiest way out for all parties concerned, aside from Joshua's, they sent him off and never looked back.

Primary-aged deaf children are dealt with by dorm staff members using a "herd mentality." As far as the staff was concerned, the children were one entity instead of individuals. This, however, worked to Joshua's advantage. In the eyes of the staff, he was not any more different than anyone else.

At first, residential school life seemed to be a preferred alternative to communicational neglect. Joshua was able to obtain some semblance of a normal childhood, being able to communicate with other children by means of newly-learned sign language.

Joshua's life at the school underwent a traumatic upheaval when he was older and placed in Mrs. Multnomah's ward. Almost immediately he was on his knees, facing the wall. Joshua's thoughts each day: Why me? I did nothing wrong. His outlook on life was that of a growing kid with dreams and ideas that were being snuffed with each passing week.

As a nine-year-old kid, he could not easily comprehend the fact he was singled out for being different from everybody else. After months of facing the wall, Joshua knew he had done no crime. He was learning the meaning of prejudice in one of the most bizarre manners possible.

After school each day, Mrs. Multnomah pointed to the hall floor when Joshua arrived. "You caused trouble," she would say, never specifying what. Eventually, Mrs. Multnomah simply glanced to the hall. Other dorm staff members deliberately avoided eye contact with him. Talking to them about Mrs. Multnomah drew blank stares.

Once, Joshua could not resist playing with the other kids outside after school. Joshua remembers how Mrs. Multnomah came storming out with the look of "evil hate" on her face, and dragging him off the sidewalk. In the basement she smashed his head against the concrete wall and said to lick the floor near the toilets.

This created a scene which would be replayed over and over in Joshua's mind long after he left the school, in the form of nightmares. Forever embedded were the mental images of cranberry-red floor tiles -- lick, lick, lick, then a slap on the back of his head, over and over again.

Mrs. Multnomah was careful. Sometimes she would wait until no one was around and, out of the blue, "trip" Joshua's leg braces to make him fall over. Then for no reason at all, she would drag Joshua to the bathroom and shove soap in his mouth, slap the back of his head and tell him he did not deserve friends.

In one instance when Joshua had a bar of soap in his mouth, he saw Mrs. Multnomah's reflection in a mop bucket, laughing. Mrs. Multnomah's "evil smirk" came to Joshua's mind every time she slapped his head against the wall.

Mrs. Multnomah had attended the other residential deaf school in the state as a deaf youngster herself. As a long-time employee, she dominated the staff with a ruthless presence of authority. She was closely related to an individual at the state department of institutions and used the connection to her advantage. Co-workers simply avoided confrontations with her.

Some former students spoke of the love and devotion she gave them, but others have described how she sometimes takes off a mask and reveals her true self.

When Joshua complained in the beginning, she would slap him in the back of his head repeatedly, banging his face on the wall as he knelt. Quickly Joshua found it to his advantage to say nothing and the endurance would be less painful.

Joshua could console himself only in the fact Mrs. Multnomah saved her most physical abuses for the retarded deaf children on her ward. The few students who were of racial minorities were also victim to Mrs. Multnomah's wrath.

14

NO DIGNITY FOR JOSHUA

When Joshua was alone, he could see Mrs. Multnomah laughing at him. She was laughing at him in his dreams. His dreams became nightmares. During his time spent in solitude he thought about revenge, devising ways to get even. But he did nothing.

After he left the school, nightmares became a way of life for Joshua. He would abruptly wake up screaming and sweating, instantly recalling specific incidents which happened to him and other students at the school.

In one instance, while the young deaf boys were lined up completely disrobed in the bathroom, awaiting a turn at the showers, some were engaged in simple horseplay. Mrs. Multnomah would not have it and promptly grabbed a paddle and directly struck a child's genitals with it. While the child was screaming in pain, she grabbed him by his hair and led him out to the hall to stand facing the wall totally naked. Still engulfed in rage, she returned to the showers, called Joshua, an innocent bystander, to come out and stand in the hall, also stark naked for all who entered the building to see.

One time when Joshua's retarded roommate fell out of bed late at night, Joshua crawled over in an attempt to help him. Mrs. Multnomah, by happenstance, walked in, grabbed his hair and dragged him to the hall. When Joshua was eventually allowed to return to bed, he noticed the roommate was still on the floor, shivering. Joshua did not dare say anything, but instead waited patiently for hours until Mrs. Multnomah went home before seeking assistance from a friendly night watchperson.

Joshua was never able to shake the false reputation of being a troublemaker and a fall guy for troubles caused by the other students. After word got around he was raped, he was falsely accused of being a homosexual, which compounded his misery and dashed any chance at normal social relationships with female students. His self-esteem and confidence were shattered. To this day, Joshua's only experience with sex was when he was raped at the school.

The first time he was raped, Joshua was in his bed asleep. When he was sexually attacked, he had virtually no idea exactly what sex was all about, but he knew he was being violated. Two older boys held him face down in bed while another raped him. Then they each took turns. They did things Joshua cannot bring himself to talk about to this day. Joshua had his first sex education lesson.

The fact nobody believed him this occurred hurt much worse than the excruciating physical pain he had endured.

Joshua found out he was not the only student being raped at the school. A slow learner, whom Joshua befriended, hinted about how he was being sexually molested by a *staff member* at the school. Afraid to even share details with Joshua, the look in his eyes told everything.

Another boy, older than Joshua, was a participant in sex games orchestrated by other students. Joshua wondered why he was so willingly cooperative in performing sexual acts for the amusement of an audience.

With much time spent kneeling in the hall, Joshua would witness dorm staff members spank other students with belts and paddles. After being taken into the dorm director's office, the children would come out crying while pulling their pants up. Although Joshua was whipped a few times himself, he had the advantage of *already* been punished.

NO DIGNITY FOR JOSHUA

Joshua often wondered why slow learners and retarded deaf children were at the school. Not only were they either abused or ignored by staff members, some *students* routinely taunted and physically abused them out in the open! It made one wonder about the physical and sexual abuse they fall victim to behind closed doors and at night.

Only a few staff members stood up to Mrs. Multnomah. Joshua saw one as a Grace from Heaven. Mrs. Larson was a relatively new staff member who worked in another dormitory. One rare occasion, she filled in for a few days for Mrs. Multnomah.

As soon as school was let out, Mrs. Larson noticed Joshua kneeling in the hall. She asked him, why are you kneeling there? I always kneel here, Joshua replied, but I don't know why. Mrs. Larson told Joshua to go out and play with the other children.

The next day, the same thing occurred. This time Mrs. Larson sat Joshua down to ask what had been happening to him. For the first time somebody was listening and Joshua cried as he explained his plight. Mrs. Larson said she would talk to one of the dorm directors and take care of this. Joshua believed he had been saved.

Later, when Mrs. Multnomah returned to work, Joshua was back in the hall again. After another week of this, Joshua began to feel cheated once again until he saw Mrs. Larson enter Mrs. Multnomah's office one afternoon. Out of the corner of his eye, he witnessed an argument of biblical proportions. It was obvious Mrs. Larson was not able to convince her superiors of Joshua's plight, but she was telling Mrs. Multnomah, *she* knew what was going on.

On her way out, she told Joshua, you have done nothing wrong, *Mrs. Multnomah* is the one with the sick mind!

17

Afterwards, Joshua would deliberately hang around where Mrs. Larson was supervising. Mrs. Multnomah would not risk a public confrontation with Mrs. Larson. Since Joshua was going to be disciplined *anyway* when he got back into his ward, he had nothing to lose. When Joshua feared imminent physical abuse, he would run to Mrs. Larson. By the time Mrs. Multnomah arrived, sometimes she would have cooled off a bit. These little victories were cherished.

After Mrs. Larson's confrontation with Mrs. Multnomah, Joshua noticed other staff members began having arguments with Mrs. Multnomah as well. Although Joshua was not sure what to make of this, he knew Mrs. Larson opened the door.

As fate would have it, Mrs. Larson passed away shortly thereafter from an illness, but Joshua was forever grateful for Grace from Heaven to have taken the time to visit him.

Later, Joshua would have dreams of crying and dreamt Mrs. Larson would hear him and comfort him back to sleep. Sometimes he felt that Mrs. Larson was his real mother.

Joshua started seeking out other friendly staff members, people who could keep an eye on him from afar. He found a few teachers to fill that need. One teacher, Mr. Kollermeier, showed concern for his well-being and attempted to rectify things. But the administrative gap between the educational side and dormitories was too wide for teachers to cross.

As the years went by, Joshua eventually ended up in the older boys' dorm away from the direct supervision of Mrs. Multnomah. But years of lies in his student file followed him. Right off the bat, a dorm staff member, Mr. Parrett, accused him of being a troublemaker and started grounding him.

Over time Mr. Parrett relented in doling out punishment for Joshua. For one thing, he noticed Joshua was not living up to the bad reputation he was supposed to have. Mr. Parrett eventually caught on to how Joshua was being used as a scapegoat by the other students and virtually left Joshua alone his last year at the school.

A high school counselor assigned to him immediately concluded Joshua's problems stemmed from the "bad" things he learned from his father. Never mind Joshua's father had been in prison since he was an infant.

Like Mr. Parrett, he eventually recorded more favorable evaluations when Joshua showed none of the traits he was reputed to have, in his files. Sadly, by that time nothing could undo what Mrs. Multnomah had done without counseling and therapy which nobody saw a need for.

Long after Joshua left Mrs. Multnomah's ward, a new student, Grant, arrived at the school, a transfer from a deaf day school. Joshua offered his help to Grant who seemed a bit out of place at the new setting, and quickly a bond between the two developed.

A ridiculous deaf school tradition, new students were hazed as Joshua put it: "Until they liked it." Joshua was well aware of the impact of such indignity and this time decided to take a stand and protect Grant from further hazing. From that point on, the friendship flourished to where Joshua was happy about at least one factor of his life; he had a true friend.

But it was not to last. Mrs. Multnomah would not have it. One day Grant said: "Stay away from me you homosexual, Mrs. Multnomah told me everything!" She had told Grant a lie, wrecking the small happiness he found. Joshua never saw Grant again, as the school year shortly came to a close and Grant transferred away.

Joshua became fixed upon Mrs. Multnomah in a way which troubled even him. Why did she go out of her way to

19

cause trouble to me now? Mrs. Multnomah was now an "evil witch polluting his mind."

The anger grew and for the first time, Joshua examined his father's pistol during a weekend trip home. The temptation to bring it to school and finish off Mrs. Multnomah was powerful. It would be easy and she deserved it.

Unable to convince himself to bring harm to Mrs. Multnomah, Joshua felt the only way to cleanse his mind was suicide, and that failed to work as well.

Joshua's hatred of Mrs. Multnomah had become an obsession, to consume much of Joshua's life. Mrs. Multnomah had made it easy for the other deaf students to belittle him, use him and mistreat him. There was no escape from his position on the deaf community social standing ladder. He held the bottom rung.

After leaving the school, Joshua moved downstate to the rural mountain countryside to live with his demons far away from the deaf and their community. He began living a life of confusion and emotional turmoil. He found some comfort in isolation, his companion from the deaf school. But he still felt Mrs. Multnomah out there, polluting his mind with unhappy thoughts in the form of nightmares.

Conversations with attorneys and counselors proved fruitless. Joshua was dismayed with the harsh reality these incidents would be difficult to prove.

The door cracked open to Joshua's private hell when a visiting missionary befriended him. Sam Sperline knew a little sign language and from afar suspected sinister things had happened to Joshua.

Sam was an advocate for disabled youngsters in the rural areas where many poor parents were simply at a loss in dealing with their disabled children. Sam Sperline saw Joshua as a young man surrounded by demons and who really did not want to be bothered, so Sam came and asked for *his* help. Sam got to know Joshua while brushing up on casual sign language conversations with him.

Joshua wore his emotions on his sleeve. Whenever the residential school was mentioned, a sneer crossed his face. Sam would then back off and change the subject.

By happenstance, Joshua mentioned Mr. Kollermeier, his favorite teacher at the residential school. Sam was astonished! He told Joshua, I *know* Mr. Kollermeier, our paths crossed many times. I did not know he was teaching at the residential deaf school. They both agreed he was a good man. For the first time, Joshua's face lit up, and Sam Sperline knew Mr. Kollermeier was the key to opening the door into Joshua's nightmare, and Sam would track him down.

A rapport developed between the two and it was a matter of time before eventually Joshua relented and let his pent-up emotions pour out like a break in a levee. Sam Sperline then confessed about having discreetly paid Mr. Kollermeier a visit.

Sam assured Joshua he learned Mrs. Multnomah was exactly as he envisioned, not an extension of his imagination, and Mr. Kollermeier was no longer at the school, having left out of frustration with the dismal conditions there.

Mr. Kollermeier told of several dorm staff member firings for physically abusing the students, and parental successes with lawsuits against the school for letting their deaf children get sexually molested by other students and staff members. Sam also learned some former students of other residential deaf schools have written books detailing many of the common occurrences Joshua initially had difficulty proving.

21

NO DIGNITY FOR JOSHUA

Mr. Kollermeier mentioned to Sam another deaf student who had, in spite of being sexually molested at the deaf school, turned his life around and become tremendously successful and widely admired. He was also a victim of Mrs. Multnomah but somehow rose above it. Mr. Kollermeier hoped Joshua would be able to do the same.

With the heavy burden now lifted, Joshua slowly returned to society. Sam suggested writing his nightmares down. Joshua started a journal and, for the first time, anxiously looked forward to the future.

Joshua is forever grateful for Sam Sperline's remarkable advice to get over Mrs. Multnomah.

Channeling his anger, Joshua was now writing to government officials. One letter to the governor prompted the school to send a social worker out to smooth things over.

But Joshua remains convinced the world has no place for residential deaf schools.

Joshua says: "I want to warn parents of the dangers at residential deaf schools. I believe residential schools should be closed and replaced with local day schools for the deaf. Our deaf children should be raised, cared for, and given advice by their own parents, whether hearing or deaf."

Today, when Joshua sees parents mistreat their kids, he cringes. Joshua often wonders about the other kids Mrs. Multnomah physically abused. Those who challenged her endured far more pain than Joshua did. Retarded children sometimes did not flinch when struck, only to get hit harder and harder. Some would not return to the school the following year, their stories never to be told.

NO DIGNITY FOR JOSHUA

WHO IS WATCHING OUR DEAF CHILDREN?

Many inside the deaf community agree, Joshua's story is just one of a thousand that could be told. The "normalcy" of this is staggering. In an attempt to explain some of the reasoning behind the dismal conditions at some of these schools, I am sharing a few insights from conversations with dorm staff members and insiders from various residential deaf schools across the country.

A seasoned staff member indicated numerous sexual abuse problems at his place of employment, including a dorm staff member who had abruptly resigned after it was disclosed she was pregnant and the father was a student at the school.

He was also amazed when a former student of the school, hired on as a teacher, carried on a relationship with a student in full view of the staff and student body. Later, this person was promoted into the school administration. In contrast, at a nearby public high school, newspaper headlines told how one teacher lost his license to teach and another dismissed for dating students.

There was a co-worker who was summoned to testify at a trial where a parent claimed both of her sons were sexually abused by a student at the school. As it turned out, this perpetrator was convicted by another court for another sexual assault and was sent to prison before the judge in this trial rendered a decision.

The capper was a horrified school nurse who abruptly resigned from her job when she was not able to get the school administration to do something about a deaf child confined to a wheelchair who kept showing up in the infirmary with evidence of having been raped.

NO DIGNITY FOR JOSHUA

A veteran employee of several residential schools indicated school administration has difficulty in finding qualified personnel to fill low-paid positions supervising deaf children. She noted alcoholics and drug abusers often find their way into these jobs. Once as she showed a new employee around campus, the person kept saying: "Oh, that looks easy," as her responsibilities were pointed out.

She pointed out budget cuts at other state agencies resulted in new staff members transferred to the school with zero deaf or educational experience. The school even waived the early childhood certificate requirement for staff members to enable hiring recent graduates of the school, after they were simply unable to fill the positions with anyone else.

She felt these conditions made the residential school fertile ground for sexual and physical abuses, especially since most parents were far away.

One told of a student approaching him desperately seeking help. It turned out a dorm director (his supervisor) was pursuing a discreet relationship with the student. The student desperately wanted it to stop but the dorm director refused to back off. Another time he stumbled upon a love affair between a student and a support-staff member, both willing participants. Such occurrences were common at his place of employment.

He mentioned an uneasy realization that by having kept quiet all these years, he had contributed to the decline of this residential school. He also wondered how anyone cannot see the tremendous moral failure of the dormitories.

And finally, an emotional staff member recalled a school out of control. Physical and sexual abuse problems were common. Morals among the staff members did not exist. The superintendent seemed unapproachable. Lawsuits were piling up against the school from disgruntled parents. Guilt-ridden staff members began purging student files. An 11-year-old student of the school had committed suicide while at home visiting parents. A new school administrator rehired an abusive staff member who was fired in a part-time capacity after the previous administration spent years trying to get her dismissed!

He vividly recalled the day he ran into an old friend, a former staff member who left the school out of frustration. He half jokingly asked if she regretted leaving the school. The former co-worker turned in the general direction of the school and gave it the universal one-fingered-salute.

CHAPTER TWO
SEXUAL ABUSE AT RESIDENTIAL DEAF SCHOOLS

Sexual abuse of children has been notoriously under-reported by the media in our society. Adults physically or sexually abuse two million children in our country every year. A million of them are raped. 2-1

Unfortunately, in segregated situations at residential deaf schools, isolated from parents and the rest of society, these incidents can only happen more frequently. Deaf children simply have not benefited from the recent public awareness on sexual abuse.

Although a large number of members of the deaf community were once victims of sexual abuse themselves at residential deaf schools, very little is said or done about this problem in the deaf community. In fact, sexual and physical abuse is *still* a significant risk for deaf children at these schools.

Experts are now saying that because of overwhelming evidence showing a high risk of sexual abuse for deaf children at residential schools, *consideration* for this should be given when the option of placing a deaf child in a residential school is discussed.

NO DIGNITY FOR JOSHUA

Researchers have concluded that deaf children were considerably more likely to be physically and sexually abused at residential schools than at a mainstream setting. They pointed out segregating deaf children during their vulnerable childhood years away from supervising parents removes some safeguards normally available to them.

Pedophiles often willingly accept poorly-paid jobs in these schools in return for "loosely structured" working conditions where predatory activity is not easily detected.

Dorm staff members and older children are the leading perpetrators with these sexual abuse attacks usually occurring in dormitories. Other employees such as bus drivers, janitors and service personnel are among those perpetrators posing a threat to children at residential deaf schools. Teachers actually accounted for very few cases. [2-2]

Not only are some residential deaf schools under investigation, experts have unequivocal evidence of sexual and physical abuses occurring at a number of other state residential deaf schools. This erases any thought that this problem is unique to only a few schools. [2-3]

It is not uncommon to read about these occurrences in the news media. Recently an investigation by state police was requested and a staff member dismissed at a state blind school in Oregon where some students are also deaf. Also, an arrest in New York of an employee who fondled a deaf-blind student there. In California, a 19-year-old male residential deaf student is on trial for allegedly raping a 17-year-old girl, also a student at the school. In Virginia, a major problem with students sexually abusing other students at the residential deaf school there has been reported, and school closure is being considered. [2-4]

NO DIGNITY FOR JOSHUA

At residential deaf schools, sexual abuse is so common it often becomes normalized. Sexual experimentation leads to sexual preference confusion which makes children vulnerable to perpetrators. This normalization triggers a vicious cycle of repetition. Children abused by adults then turn around and abuse younger children.

One expert described the shocking emotional problems of one deaf female. After graduation from a residential deaf school, she found herself unable to cope with life outside of the school and eventually told of her experiences to sexual abuse researchers.

As it turned out, she was sexually abused at the school to the point where it became normalized. She did not consider the sexual contacts with the adult staff at the school as abusive, but rather, supportive. Now having left the school, she told of feeling "empty," since she had no one to communicate and have sex with.

Experts hear comments from deaf children, either as abuser or victim, such as: 'I didn't know sex with sister is wrong; no one told me...'

Therapists also point out: 'Whom would they tell? And how?' One of the problems is very little sexual abuse awareness material is written specifically for deaf children. Because of this, an abused deaf person thinks this happens everywhere, gives up and accepts that it is "part of life." [2-5]

Some occurrences at residential deaf schools even defy explanation, such as the case of a high school female transferring to the residential deaf school from a mainstream setting. On her first day at the school, some of the other *students* cut out the crotch on all of her clothes and filled her private bathtub with red dye and left a butcher knife in the tub for her to find.

Counselors for the deaf are saying deaf sexual abuses are their leading concern. One confessed nearly all of her female deaf clients were abused at residential schools by staff members.

In a surprising discovery, researchers report sexually abused deaf males account for the majority of deaf sexual abuse victims, while females are not too far behind. By comparison, in the mainstream society, female children are four times as likely to be victim of sexual abuse. This indicates concern for possible victimizing should be given to *both* male and female deaf children. [2-6]

Deaf children are preyed upon by others, partly because of the child's lack of ability to communicate. The overwhelming majority of sexual abusers are known to the victim, with the majority of sexual abuse incidents occurring more than once, usually a number of times over a few years. [2-7]

Laws currently in place to protect children are sometimes being circumvented. For example, it appears a state law in one state which *forbids* rehiring of dismissed staff members permits rehiring for part-time positions.

This legal loophole returned a number of fired personnel back to supervising children, including a staff member forced into early retirement for abusing smaller children who legally returned to supervise older children.

A few in the deaf community are recognizing the severity of these problems and are speaking out, seeking solutions.

In an informal survey conducted by a deaf community-oriented periodical, a large number of respondents indicated a problem of unreported sexual abuse at residential schools. Others have heard stories from deaf acquaintances who have attended residential schools. [2-8]

A university professor recalled when she was a teacher at a deaf school, she was puzzled why some females were chronically late for class and their faces were sheet-white. Eventually she found out they were sexually taken advantage of by a deaf staff member, whom they feared and were afraid to report. [2-9]

Numerous other members of the deaf community are willing to admit privately of these sinister things occurring at residential deaf schools when they were students. One needs only to ask. Guidance from most culturally-deaf leaders is absent, leaving many at a loss where to begin.

The few who have come forward are asking for leaders of the deaf community to take action to counter these sexual abuse problems at residential deaf schools.

Some note a vital need to break this vicious cycle where victims of abuse grow up to become abusers themselves. They also ask parents to listen to their children to see if this abuse is happening. Parents often believe these things do not occur. [2-10]

SUMMARY

I have previously touched on incidents of sexual abuse at residential deaf schools and in the deaf community. However since then, numerous sources have indicated it is even more common and prevalent than I thought. More than that, these widespread incidents are *still going on!*

A number of us feel the problem of sexual abuse at residential deaf schools is so out of control, parents should consider this reason enough to not *ever* consider a residential school option for deaf children.

The residential school is confronted with two challenges it is seemingly having little success in dealing with:

One, it would seem simple enough, is keeping the staff under control. Alleged or actual, residential schools are faring very poorly. The other is the problem of student-to-student sexual abuse.

There is an element of trust involved when a student is placed in a residential school far from the eyes of the parents. When that trust has been violated, we are seeing angry parents jerk their children out of these schools and start filing numerous lawsuits.

Culturally-deaf leaders are doing next to nothing. They are actually engulfed in larger debates about Miss America's mode of communication than any concern for sexual abuse of deaf children.

A writer from Great Britain confessed the feeling of many culturally-deaf leaders here when she said: "So what? Sexual abuse occurs everywhere. It's nothing new, we're used to it." Many of us would prefer to keep our deaf children at home and keep an eye on their upbringing rather than entrust them to people having this frame of mind.

I recently had a conversation with a culturally-deaf person who considered writing about her sexual abuse problems at a residential school. She was discouraged by the leaders of the deaf community with a subtle threat saying it would only serve to *harm the deaf community and serve no useful purpose!*

A culturally-deaf activist underlined the whole issue by pointing out there is not a single culturally-deaf person who can say he does not know of any sexually-abused culturally-deaf person.

Further, a culturally-deaf oriented newspaper recently published an editorial commenting on physical and sexual abuse in the deaf community. The writer, an advocate for the deaf, stated "I can honestly say I don't know of one deaf or hard-of-hearing woman who has not been assulted at least once." He wonders why this "culture of abuse" exists and suggests perhaps deaf people are afraid to speak out in fear of deaf militants among the culturally-deaf leadership. He pointed out those who had contrary views often suffered verbal, and even physical abuse from these militants. 2-11

One state overwhelmed with the problems of sexual abuse at residential deaf schools is seriously considering *abolishing* these schools as the best possible solution. Some on the board of education there feel giving parents of deaf children vouchers to send them elsewhere is preferred to the state being in the sex-policing business.

As a truly sad testimonial to all this, there have been a number of pro-culturally-deaf books written by culturally-deaf leaders and hearing sympathizers, published in recent years for the most part, aimed at coaxing hearing parents of deaf children to send their children to residential deaf schools. In most cases, *not one word* is said about the extreme danger of sexual abuse these children will face at these schools and later on in the deaf community. Nor are these problems addressed and solutions brought forth. Such writers should feel guilty for recklessly endangering innocent children by not disclosing this horrible truth to the parents.

Culturally-deaf leaders *must* be made to understand this normalcy of sexual abuse is *not* tolerable in our society. If solutions hasten the demise of deaf culture, so be it.

CHAPTER THREE
THE MILITANTS AND
A CULTURE FRACTURED

MILITANCY AND INFIGHTING

Militancy in the deaf community is on the increase, especially among students and some staff members at Gallaudet University. These militants' extreme activities have provoked outraged public reaction from both deaf and hearing.

Despite the appearance of a united front, culturally-deaf leaders are severely fragmented, not even agreeing who does and does not belong to deaf culture.

While the deaf community comprises only ten percent of the total number of deaf people, the militants have outraged the other ninety percent by trampling on their rights and forcing their own values on them. [3-1]

Some have noted these militants have an 'organized campaign to interfere with the rights of parents of deaf infants,' and insist all deaf children belong to the deaf community, not to their hearing parents!

These militants have also left the impression on readers of recent articles on deafness that they speak for the majority of deaf people, when actually, as one deaf observer noted, "Nothing could be farther from the truth!" [3-2]

NO DIGNITY FOR JOSHUA

It has been said these leaders are often guilty of "wrapping issues under the cultural diversity banner" as a means of obtaining legitimacy. 3-3

Not all culturally-deaf people are buying the militant deaf agenda. There are many rational people within the deaf community who understand a need for diversity. In fact, some are so disillusioned and deeply offended, they are seeking alternative lifestyles.

For instance, a third generation deaf of deaf man who was raised in the deaf community, having a parent who taught at a residential deaf school, publicly disavowed the culturally-deaf way of life in a newspaper editorial. He chose a Cochlear Implant for his deaf infant son and placed a value on utilizing speech skills, something the deaf community considers as a negative value. He also predicted technology may end deaf culture, a statement which has been echoed by many others. 3-4

There is also concern of self-defeating idiosyncrasies of deaf culture. A commonly used metaphor within the deaf community: If one crab is strong enough to climb out of the barrel, others will pull him back in. 3-5

Culturally-deaf oriented organizations, such as the National Association of the Deaf (NAD), are coming under fire of late. Some culturally-deaf individuals are objecting to the NAD leadership's way of attempting to speak for *all* deaf people. Many are not pleased the NAD thinks their problems are insignificant, and actually would appreciate progress to ease the burden of deafness. 3-5

Deaf militant activity has led some to note that classification as a deaf person nowadays is often akin to opening a Pandora's box of controversy. 3-6

It is virtually impossible for parents to even choose a method of educating a deaf child without eventually offending someone somewhere over a personal decision they made for their own child.

Culturally-deaf leaders are also concerned about attempts to eliminate deaf culture, despite the fact no governmental action can forbid deaf people living life as they choose. Nevertheless, a great number of culturally-deaf people still view hearing people as oppressors, usually resulting in their not wanting anything to do with hearing people.

Militant deaf rhetoric has led to backlash. One example: A nationally renowned pro-oral organization undertook a *freedom of choice* campaign targeted at parents of deaf children to counter pressure from culturally-deaf militants on parents of deaf children.

A writer speaking out on governmental action to preserve any kind of culture said: "...when it takes a law to enforce a culture, that culture is already dead -- and no legislation can save it."

And finally, in defiance to enormous pressure from militant deaf leaders, one culturally-deaf professor commented: "*Nothing can reduce me to a gibbering goon.*" [3-7]

A NEED FOR UNITY

"*We must all hang together or assuredly we shall hang separately.*" One deaf writer aptly quoted Benjamin Franklin, whose comments apply very smartly to the current situation among the deaf. These lines in the sand, such as the culturally-deaf, orally-deaf, late-deafened adults, the hard-of-hearing, including in recent years the CI-deaf and mainstream-educated deaf goes to show the unifying task at hand.

Commentary ranging from, "Sometimes even the most trivial differences between otherwise similar groups give rise to fierce rivalry," to "the emergence of 'deaf culture' parallels the rise of hard-core multiculturism that defines people in terms of race, gender, ethnicity or sexual preference," indicate the degree of the division faced by deaf leaders in any unifying effort. 3-8

Many culturally-deaf people identify themselves as users of sign language and frown upon any use of speech. Some may even "mock and jeer" those who use speech in addition to sign language when communicating, leading one deaf writer to make a historical comparison of this behavior to some African-Americans during the pre-war slavery period in the South, where "house slaves" conducted themselves in a manner to maintain their "superiority" over "field slaves."

All this underlines the *special urgency* of the circumstances deaf people find themselves in at this point in history. Some are afraid the world will care less for our special needs as a result of this bickering and feel the few vocal people who believe in a mythical "purity" of separatism destroy the financial and social rewards of unity. 3-9

Interestingly, the rejection of the non-culturally deaf by many members of the deaf community is not unique to the United States. In Great Britain, there are descriptions of the deaf community being like a "closed shop" and "unwelcoming."

This has led some people to wonder how they can work for equal rights and opportunities for the deaf in the mainstream society when non-culturally deaf are not even allowed their rights within the deaf community. 3-10

NO DIGNITY FOR JOSHUA

SELF-DEFEATING TENDENCIES AND OTHER AREAS DESERVING OF IMPROVEMENT

One disgusted editor noted how it has become a national pastime in the deaf community to air dirty laundry in the press. Some have wondered what is a parent to think when reading such things? [3-11]

We are also seeing more anonymous letters published by some deaf-related publications, serving no purpose but to spark rumors and aggravate readers. Has anybody ever heard of being *friendly adversaries?*

Appreciation is given to editors who called for the identification of anonymous mudslingers and character assassins. Shame to those editors who actually carried out personal mudslinging *in their own editorial sections!*

At a national-level meeting dealing with issues related to deafness, the invited representative from the deaf community, a professor of deaf studies, made it obvious he did not care to attend or listen to any of the other speakers' sessions. In addition, he committed a cardinal sin by deferring tough questions from the audience to a *hearing sympathizer!* This made all of us deaf people look inept.

This speaker later commented on not being quite prepared for an onslaught from a hostile audience. This was a clear case where years of militant rhetoric returned to haunt culturally-deaf leaders.

A seemingly acceptable and subtle form of bigotry is common in the deaf community with very little effort underway to correct the problem. Deaf individuals who are not culturally-deaf are looked down upon. While this has been the case for a century, what is newly disturbing is the attitude toward late-deafened adults (LDA's), who are often rejected for being less than "real" deaf people. [3-12]

The LDA's are becoming a force to be reckoned with. Many in the deaf community disagree totally with the LDA ideology and fear they will usurp some of the clout the deaf community has enjoyed for years. This is a new dilemma for culturally-deaf leaders who have already gone on record refusing to share power with other factions, especially any oral-based factions.

Compared to the culturally-deaf, the LDA's have the advantage of having an unlimited number of potential members. Since they are actively organizing, it is only a matter of time before they establish themselves as a new *deaf majority*, displacing the leaders of the deaf culture. Culturally-deaf leaders only have themselves to blame if their concerns fall by the wayside.

To complicate matters for the deaf militants, another "enemy" has emerged. As more and more people opt for the Cochlear Implant, these recipients will also outnumber the culturally-deaf and will gravitate toward the more appealing LDA ideology, effectively shutting out the culturally-deaf leadership.

Members of the deaf community have a tendency to discriminate among themselves by assigning each other to a rung on a "deaf social standing" ladder, often hampering personal development. Labels attached to deaf children during early years at residential deaf schools remain affixed to them for life, regardless of how erroneous.

For example: One culturally-deaf person referred to a prominent deaf manager of a state agency as "not being very smart." Upon inquiry why this was so, it was because she was assigned to the "B" class at the residential deaf school, not the apparently much more elite "A" class. This relegated her to one of the lower class deaf not to be included in many deaf social functions. Never mind she had a Master's degree and the person making the comment was unemployed and receiving disability benefits.

As the years went by, the deaf manager rode the ranks to the top, surpassing many hearing peers and eventually became director at a deaf educational facility. Yet, her accomplishments impressed few within the deaf community and many actually chose to avoid her program.

This also works in reverse. Deaf students who were looked up to as leaders in school, will always have the "leadership-aura" later in life, even if they drop out of college and live on disability benefits indefinitely.

Many in the deaf community are guilty of virtually ignoring the deaf-blind. They do not appear to want to take the time to communicate with the deaf-blind using tactile sign language. One deaf man who became blind later in life said the onset of blindness was easier to take than being ignored by what were formerly his friends. 3-13

POLITICALLY CORRECT TERMINOLOGY

Culturally-deaf leaders are using newly developed, "politically-correct" terminology as a public relations ploy. Newer examples include: Deaf children are a *social minority*, they should be *treasured*. Another word is *genocide*, the weapon of choice among many deaf militants, applied to anything and everything that could prevent a child from becoming or remaining deaf.

Bottom line: Political word games are not helping little deaf Johnny and Jane read any better.

NO DIGNITY FOR JOSHUA

In recent years, many culturally-deaf writers have been using an upper-case "D" when using the word *deaf* to describe a culturally-deaf person. (For example; the Deaf man.)

Lower-cased "d" would be used to describe a person who was deaf but did not subscribe to the deaf culture notion. (Such as, the orally-educated deaf man.)

This big D, little d, concept is not normal English protocol, but since many culturally-deaf people do not place too much value on English these days, one should not be surprised. Unfortunately, there are proposals to *officially* adopt these changes which could find their way into the English language. 3-14

There are a number of problems with the whole big D, little d concept.

First, the obvious: Most people selected at random from our society will have no idea what the writer is referring to, reading material utilizing the big D, little d concept.

Second, what does one do when a sentence is begun with the word *deaf* which should *always* be capitalized?

Third, how is a writer to know which case of "d" to use when the political inclination of a deaf person is unknown? Does the writer risk offending that person one way or another by making an assumption? Or do culturally-deaf leaders suggest we add either "little d's" or "big D's" after our names (much like the current affiliation of political parties to our elected officials)?

Fourth, it is a subtle argument for the existence of a deaf culture. Also, it draws a clear line of distinction between the culturally-deaf and all other deaf factions, once again using the Us vs. Them line of thinking by the militant deaf which serves to harm *all* deaf individuals.

Fifth, how does one distinguish between a big D and little d when one is speaking or signing?

And finally, it is bad enough when there are so many exceptions to the rules of proper English usage, to make it the more difficult to learn by the deaf, without throwing in a few more exceptions of their own.

Let us keep it simple. If a deaf writer wants to indicate a person is a member of the deaf community, use *culturally-deaf*. This way there is no doubt in any reader's mind what the writer is saying. We probably should not be dividing ourselves into factions anyway.

MUCH ADO ABOUT NOTHING

When a deaf person recently won the Miss America pageant, the leaders of the deaf community were not particularly pleased, as she was *orally-deaf*. The winner was subject to a year of torment from these culturally-deaf leaders criticizing every move she made. Never mind she represented ninety percent of deaf individuals who are not part of deaf culture and the fact she tried to be accommodating to *all* deaf people.

Instead of her positively raising public awareness for all of us, we found many culturally-deaf leaders attacking her for using her voice instead of using sign language. Even an official at Gallaudet University was quoted as saying: "A lot of us feel that she shouldn't represent us to the mainstream world!" [3-15]

Please! She won a beauty contest, not an elected political office! Judging from the way this incident was played out in newspaper headlines, leaders of the deaf community tarnished both sign language and deaf people with this senseless bickering.

41

NO DIGNITY FOR JOSHUA

Leaders of the deaf community are also raising a ruckus about Hollywood movie production companies using hearing actors to portray deaf roles in films. They are demanding *only* deaf individuals are to portray these deaf roles.

I will not get into the implications of this being *reverse* discrimination; however there are two major points that need to be weighed into all of this. In the first place, aren't actors who perform in motion picture roles *actors*? The other item is; big Hollywood productions are privately funded *(and highly speculative gambles at that)*. There is no public money entailed here. Why are we taking this time to make a big fuss in telling one group of investors how to invest their money?

Hollywood has a long history of miscasting roles anyway, and if producers do not want to use what seems to be an obvious choice, the deaf probably do not want to be associated with that production. Forcing things down producers' throats will not win us friends. Besides, with all the public outrage from the deaf, heaven forbid they should ever consider producing and funding a script with deaf roles in it again!

Unfortunately, there is a capper for this. The NAD, the largest advocacy organization for the deaf, has recently voted to make this controversy a *national priority!* Doesn't our society have other issues and causes more worthy and deserving of the time and energy? 3-16

THINGS GOING RIGHT IN THE DEAF COMMUNITY

Gallaudet University recently undertook an ambitious plan to reverse the severe problem of student illiteracy. This plan was put together after some professors at Gallaudet who were frustrated at the students' poor English skills stopped giving writing assignments.

NO DIGNITY FOR JOSHUA

On an unrelated matter, the current deaf president of Gallaudet has stated that the Gallaudet community must accept *cultural diversity* for the university to effectively serve deaf and hard of hearing students. 3-17

In a brave move, a culturally-deaf oriented publication disclosed some of the crude tactics employed by militant deaf leaders. Calling it an example of 'deaf trashing other deaf,' they publicly challenged these perpetrators to identify themselves.

Some culturally-deaf leaders are *finally* recognizing that many residential deaf school graduates have no career direction, are facing social problems, failing with emotional challenges, and are having independent living problems.

With this admission, we have cleared a hurdle. Perhaps now solutions can be effectively proposed, even if it means a diminished importance for residential schools.

Some have noted a "historic shift" in the attitudes of many within the deaf community. They believe the onset of modern technology has triggered a "new breed" of deaf people as the dividing line between hearing and deaf starts to fade. They note the "traditionalists," supporting the old ways of segregation and isolation from the hearing society, are not particularly pleased. 3-18

When one school district selected SEE (Signed Exact English) for use in classrooms with deaf and hard-of-hearing children, members of the deaf community worked with the district leaders to incorporate ASL features and modify some signs used.

Originally outraged that ASL was not selected, they found having a team approach worked. While not everybody was pleased, culturally-deaf leaders agree positive changes have occurred and the SEE being utilized here seems closer to ASL since their input was heeded. 3-19

In a dramatic about face, one prominent leader of the culturally-deaf who is also a top state government official, is attempting to close a residential deaf school notorious for failure of its students to succeed after graduation.

The fact eighty percent of the recent graduates from that residential school were dependent on Social Security is helping ease his decision to make this drastic change. He has however, faced the wrath of culturally-deaf leaders even though there are others who say if there is anyone who knows what is best for the deaf community, he's the one.

Ingenious culturally-deaf people are finding ways to fight discrimination without resorting to ADA claims and lawsuits.

For example, after a hospital refused to provide an interpreter, a deaf patient reluctantly signed a release form for an emergency surgery, but added a statement there was no interpreter, in order to put the liability back on to the hospital.

An uproar ensued and the hospital administrator finally agreed to provide an interpreter after realizing the deaf patient was right. 3-20

Culturally-deaf people are fighting back against sexual harassment. Not only are lawsuits being filed, but courts are awarding monetary damage. The 9th U.S. Court of Appeals rendered a decision in favor of a deaf worker whose hearing supervisor, the only manager knowing sign language and having knowledge of deaf community customs, used her deafness to satisfy his sexual needs.

As an interesting sidelight, the supervisor in question was eventually caught allegedly sexually abusing *another* employee in a sting set up by the employee's union officials!

Deaf sexual abuse victims are even starting to bring criminal charges against deaf perpetrators. One example: An all-deaf rape trial, a case where the accused, victim and all the witnesses were deaf. Both the prosecution and the defense attorneys took steps to ensure fairness in a trial where everything had to be interpreted. 3-21

A UNIFIED DEAF SUCCESS STORY

Closed Captioning (or CC) on television has been universally appreciated by all deaf factions, a clear example of the prizes of a unified front.

The ability of being able to absorb information on an equal basis as a hearing person without the feeling of having to be "dependent" on another person such as an interpreter is god-sent. In fact, many of us prefer to watch a CC version of a lecture or speech rather than utilizing a "live" interpreter.

An unexpected side benefit was the utilization of CC by many people with literacy problems and immigrants learning English, as well as children learning to read. CC has been known to be used in public places where noisy backgrounds prevent normal listening, as well as in places where noise levels must be kept low.

I once heard a radio sports talk show host mention how CC was the greatest thing to ever hit sports radio. It was now possible for him to host a live sports call-in show and follow multiple sporting events on separate television sets all at the same time.

Consumers must insist *all* video and broadcast programs be closed captioned. A large number of recent nontheatrical releases, many cable programs and home videos are still not being captioned. Even the ACLU has supported requiring *all* cable and broadcast signals be closed-captioned.

To have television and video programs CC`d is not expensive. Producers should be aware that CC on programs have become as desired as sound was to film back in the early days of movie making. 3-22

CHAPTER FOUR
THE FIERY DEAF LANGUAGE AND EDUCATION ISSUES

EFFORTS TO PRESERVE ASL, A LOST CAUSE?

Hardly anybody will dispute the great divide of biblical proportions between proponents of *English*-based sign languages and those supporting ASL (American Sign Language). There is all kinds of infighting among linguists and others foraying into this fiery issue.

There is also a division within the ranks of ASL supporters. One of the characteristics of language in general is that it evolves along with the society using it. This has some saying if ASL is a true language, it must evolve like any other language. Others steadfastly believe ASL must be preserved *exactly* the way it is today.

The ASL preservationists hope to prevent ASL from being influenced by new types of deaf individuals. They fear the hard-of-hearing, the mainstreamed-deaf, late-deafened adults, and even hearing people using ASL may wreak havoc with their language.

On the other side of the coin, with this new "outside" influence, ASL will evolve to being a lot closer to English than it is today. In the end it can be viewed as a way for all the factions of deaf people to reach a common denominator.

If the ASL preservationists should somehow succeed in enacting measures to prevent ASL from evolving, one must wonder whether it might eventually fall into disuse by most deaf people in favor of other types of signed languages having fewer encumbrances. Much of the popularity of ASL stems from the "freedom" from the rules of English. To create new "rules and compliance criteria" for ASL will diminish the appeal of ASL for many.

Another factor is that the number of human languages is rapidly declining, with perhaps only as few as 250 of the existing 6000 languages surviving the next 100 years. All things considered, these preservationists may have very little chance of *successfully* preventing ASL from evolving. 4-1

ASL VS ENGLISH-BASED SIGN LANGUAGES

Against conventional wisdom, ASL-only proponents have somehow managed to establish a degree of credibility among many in our society even though the benefits of an English-based language of signs are obvious.

ASL is a unifying bond among many deaf, and many simply will not let it go. Unfortunately, ASL proponents have also sunk to mudslinging and personal attacks on culturally-deaf supporters of English.

An outspoken deaf author has said we should not get confused about two separate issues regarding ASL, *legitimacy* and *utility*. He believes it may be possible ASL is a distinct language, and perhaps an identifying factor, but it is nearly useless outside the deaf community. Deaf individuals with additional skills of communication will have a distinct advantage.

Culturally-deaf leaders have contended that ASL needs to be learned before English. Since most textbooks are in English, as there is no written form of ASL, this writer raises the question of how one learns to read English in order to read a textbook on ASL?

While this writer is an ardent supporter of the oral approach, his arguments bolster the strength of an English-based sign language. Culturally-deaf opponents generally disagree, but have conceded he is right on a number of items, including a need to devise ways the deaf can succeed in mainstream society and improve their reading and writing skills. [4-2]

Leaders of the deaf community are also proponents of a new way of educating the deaf called the Bi-Bi (for Bi-lingual, Bi-cultural) approach. However, this appears to be more of a scheme to comply with "political correctness" than any revolutionary new educational concept.

At first glance, Bi-Bi appears to include more English, but it is actually utilized only secondarily, with very little or no importance placed on spoken English. Bi-Bi advocates also tend to be vague exactly how the deaf child will learn English. Some deaf educators are sure it will not happen by itself, and many avoid talking about this issue. [4-3]

Upon close examination, Bi-Bi appears to be old methods rehashed, only this time with a more appealing and politically-safe label. Many of us urge this approach be scrutinized further.

Many hearing experts and deaf people who support English as a first language are concerned about many culturally-deaf leaders pushing for less English and more ASL being taught as a solution to poor English reading skills in deaf children. They fear these actions will only further segregate the deaf from the mainstream and lead to stronger dependence on deaf culture.

Others feel these endless discussions and debates on ASL vs English may limit parental options. They believe a wide variety of methods is needed, as at present, to serve each unique and different deaf child. [4-4]

One prominent culturally-deaf leader once stated: "...the validity of ASL has been accepted," and "When our language was acknowledged, we gained our freedom." Many of us ask: Acknowledged by whom? Freedom from what? Hearing tyranny? There was no profound revelation in our society whenever this event supposedly occurred. [4-5]

These culturally-deaf leaders (who are usually "deaf of deaf," meaning deaf individuals who have culturally-deaf parents) may have succeeded in pulling off a huge marketing scheme on the American public, mostly fooling only those who want to believe such a separate deaf language actually exists.

This same person, this time referring to her knowledge and mastery of ASL, also stated: "There are many things that I can experience for which you (hearing people) have no equivalent." We should not forget it works both ways and I for one, being deaf of deaf, and having a 30-year mastery of ASL, first acquired at a residential deaf school, would not hesitate to trade my mastery of ASL to experience *what the hearing can, for which the deaf have no equivalent.*

Pro-English activists are publicly speaking out, decrying the crude tactics used by deaf militants. One has said: 'They see nothing wrong with using methods belittling the U.S. Constitution and the Bill of Rights to hush all opponents of 'pure ASL.' If the public were actually aware of the tactics used, the credibility of these militant leaders would evaporate overnight.' [4-6]

There are also concerns lest extreme actions of these militants could bring a rise to oralism. Many non-culturally-deaf adults may be offended enough to avoid any association with the deaf community, of which sign language is the most visible flag. Already, some oral-deaf leaders have publicly disclosed how plenty disgusted they are with the deaf militants.

Anti-English proposals from the deaf community have even made their way into congressional and state legislative committees. Militants have proposed legislation requiring *all* deaf children use ASL in classrooms, regardless of the lack of evidence showing ASL to be a better method of education. So far, no such proposals have yet succeeded in becoming law. [4-7]

Politicians must be aware these culturally-deaf lobbyists do not always represent all deaf factions. Otherwise we would end up with most deaf-related legislation written from the viewpoint of militants.

The most glaring weakness in the argument for ASL as a separate language is the lack of a written form for it. In an apparent attempt to rectify this, a culturally-deaf committee has undertaken the task of developing symbols for each sign. [4-8]

Many of us are not sure what they hope to accomplish. Tossing aside what little English many deaf people know, coming up with a whole *new* written language just to answer critics cannot possibly be beneficial to deaf children.

Deaf children have a hard enough time mastering English already without a need for other language-related topics to crowd the classroom plate.

Written symbols will be learned by very few and will be difficult to decipher generations from now. Sign language and ASL is better preserved on videotape.

Among sign language users, most use a variation of an English-based sign language such as SEE. (Signed Exact English). Only a small percentage actually use "pure" ASL. A large number of deaf people are keeping ties to the mainstream world by signing in SEE, the language of our society. Many also view SEE as a bridge uniting the deaf and the hearing. Some reports indicate a higher level of English skills after SEE was implemented among students who were previously strictly oral educated. [4-9]

Nobody is actively proposing sign language be eliminated. But many culturally-deaf people are fearful anyway and this has led one culturally-deaf leader to comment: "More often than not, hearing people view sign language as an evil, so to speak, that must be eradicated so the deaf can participate in the hearing world..."

It is critical some form of sign language survive. Some staunch pro-oral supporters will concede for some deaf people, speechreading is simply not possible.

Sign language is also less of a threat to spoken English than many believe. A recent study shows sign language actually helps improve lipreading skills and spoken language is not threatened. [4-10]

While culturally-deaf leaders have recently succeeded in obtaining a small rise in the number of deaf schools using ASL, it is only a hollow victory, as there are suggestions the total number of deaf schools and programs using any kind of sign language in general (including ASL) has registered a significant drop. For one reason or another, sign language as a primary teaching method for deaf children appears to be declining. 4-11

This ominous development should bolster culturally-deaf leaders into reassessing priorities or, as the trend shows, some day there may not be any sign languages left to preserve.

THE CASE FOR ENGLISH

Internationally, the deaf and hearing alike regard English as our world's *lingua franca*. They find it incomprehensible militant deaf leaders are disregarding the importance of the world's *international language*. 4-6

Another argument for one language is the unifying force. Examples abound in our world today in Bosnia, the former Soviet Union, and even in Quebec, where we see homelands in turmoil over bilingual and ethnic differences.

Interestingly, a number of immigrants from India, Chile and Hungary have asked Congress to declare English as the United States`s official language saying they did not come here to preserve their language and culture at governmental expense. They believe English is a unifying factor and is a small price to pay for the benefits of being part of this society. 4-12

Time and time again, it has been noted that the basis for success in our society is one's ability to read and write English. English ties our country's social, business and educational fabric together. The degree of one's fluency in English determines one's ability to succeed in these three areas.

The culturally-deaf leaders' movement for the devaluation of English in favor of ASL is not unanimous. Prominent leaders in the deaf community have for years spoken out in support of English and some see no reason why deaf people cannot master *both* English and ASL. 4-13

DEAF STUDIES AND DEAF LINGUISTICS

Culturally-deaf leaders are horrified very few culturally-deaf students are actually studying sign linguistics and deaf studies. They fear some day the majority of the people knowing more about deaf culture and sign language will be hearing. [4-14]

This brings to mind the burning question of exactly how many culturally-deaf individuals are fully educated in the deaf language issues being debated today, or whether this ASL-as-a-language movement is a result of orchestration by only a few key culturally-deaf leaders?

One linguistics researcher revealed that by supporting English-based sign languages, he is not eligible for any grants. However, by claiming to be an ASL proponent, he can get teaching and research monies. [4-6]

Outraged deaf leaders have decried these linguists researching ASL as a pitiful lot who completely depend on grants, seemingly serving no other purpose. Questions have been raised perhaps ASL was *created* and is now being researched by some for no other purpose than to ensure it continues to exist.

Discussions have revealed that job openings for people with deaf-studies degrees are actually rather limited and comparatively low paying. In addition, job security depends on the whims of voters, as nearly all positions are publicly funded. In addition, recent activity by deaf militants has left a bad taste in many taxpayers' minds and they may be hesitant to fund or consider new programs for the deaf.

Ultimately, with a perhaps dwindling number of culturally-deaf people expected in the future, a need for such expertise would diminish except for utilization in a historical context.

NO DIGNITY FOR JOSHUA

As an interesting sidelight, demands from the militant leaders requiring all teachers of the deaf to take mostly deaf-studies courses as part of continuing education has resulted in many frustrated teachers leaving the profession. [4-7]

RESIDENTIAL DEAF SCHOOLS, ANCIENT RELICS

While many proponents of these residential schools argue that the same shortcomings may be found in mainstream schools, this is exactly the point I am trying to make. Parents of deaf children must be aware no utopia exists for deaf children. The recent disclosures of sexual abuse problems at residential deaf schools is a somber testimonial to this.

The educational output at these schools has historically been poor. Research evidence clearly indicates a huge disadvantage of an education at a residential school compared to nearly all other methods of educating the deaf.

Some are now publicly calling for discontinuing the *warehousing* approach to educating the deaf typically found at residential schools. They are also saying residential schools should *not* be a replacement for families and they should provide an education superior to public schools. [4-15]

Since nearly all residential school graduates fail to *even approach* public school standards, and compounded with the moral failures, one must ask why have residential deaf schools at all?

Another consideration is the cost to society for residential deaf schools. In one state it costs $9,000 to educate a normal hearing child from K to 12th grade. The cost to educate a deaf child in a mainstream setting is $44,000. At a residential school: $429,000.

If the culturally-deaf leaders were to have their way and educate *all* deaf children at residential schools, it would cost our society $420 *billion* per year. [4-16]

Many of us applaud the Clinton Administration for not buckling to culturally-deaf leaders' demands for more segregated deaf schools. In reaction to this, one superintendent of a deaf school said: "It is a terrible abuse." [4-17]

A FEW RESIDENTIAL SCHOOL ANECDOTES

Everything that is wrong with residential deaf schools can be summed up in this one incident that occurred when a friend of mine was just about ready to graduate from a residential deaf school.

He recalled being engaged in a casual conversation with the school bus driver and gardener, who happened to be hearing and popular with the students.

When asked about his upcoming plans after graduation, my friend said: "I want to write books." The deaf school bus driver chuckled as he replied: "No, deaf people *CANNOT* write books!"

Recently, a construction contractor happened to be visiting a residential deaf school when he found school workmen illegally removing all the old asbestos insulation from plumbing pipes in a student dormitory. While the workmen wore minimal protection, there was *no* attempt to protect or shield the deaf children from breathing the harmful, cancer-causing fiber dust being strewn about. Although the degree of danger of abestos is still debated, it is better to be safe than sorry. Wisdom most parents possess does not exist here.

Someone told me how her parents respectfully heeded the advice of their family doctor who told them to just send her away to a residential school after discovering she was deaf.

Her parents then made plans to have a close relative living near the school check in on their five-year-old daughter

56

from time to time to maintain some level of a family experience for her. However, the school quickly put an end to this family tie by calling it "disruptive," and told them to save the visits for the child's monthly weekend visit home.

Diversity is a foreign word at some residential deaf schools. At one such school, the superintendent's sister and her husband were on the teaching staff, his brother and his spouse on the dorm staff, another brother's spouse on the teaching staff. The superintendent's own wife worked part time. One dorm director had his spouse on the payroll as well as a daughter in the teaching section and a son working part time. Another dorm director also had his spouse on the staff. Two other married couples were on the teaching staff and one woman with a son and his wife, all dorm staff members. All were culturally-deaf, at a school with fewer than 250 students. Nepotism like this exists at Gallaudet University as well.

I recently ran across some old enrollment evaluation documents from the residential deaf school I was sent to. It was criteria the superintendent had put together for the staff at the school to utilize to evaluate possible future students. Successful use of speech, hearing aids and progress in mainstream schools, all of which applied to me, were beyond the scope of this residential school and such students would *not* benefit from an education there. Needless to say, this directive was unheeded by the staff in my case.

MAINSTREAMING

The widespread trend today of mainstreaming, often described as *full inclusion*, the placement of deaf children in their local schools, is vehemently opposed by deaf community leaders. However, they have admitted this is a popular movement supported by many deaf educators, administrators and parents and has attracted large numbers of deaf children.

Some professors at Gallaudet have indicated their mainstreamed-educated students usually have a better command of English skills than their counterparts educated at residential schools. There are many published reports of successful mainstream settings.

One example: Visitors at a program with thirty five deaf and hard-of hearing students are impressed with the number of both hearing and deaf students as well as staff members using sign language openly. There were also a number of interpreters on the staff to ensure deaf children were not left out of activities out of the classroom and incidental occurrences such as PA announcements. The presence of many volunteers and parents established a caring and supportive atmosphere in this successful program. [4-18]

Leaders of the deaf community would be wise to use their expertise to work with each local school district and inform on the needs of deaf children, to ensure that *all* schools attempting to educate the deaf are providing *early* language development regardless of the method. They can also ensure that sign language is still used and help eliminate other communication barriers.

Many parents who are choosing mainstreaming do not intend to hurt the deaf community. One Jewish doctor made the comparison of how he chose to send his (normal) children to a public school instead of a Jewish school based upon the lifestyle they planned to have, not as an attempt to hurt Jewish society. [4-19]

ALTERNATIVE METHODS OF EDUCATING THE DEAF

The successes with Cued Speech seem to be overshadowed by political activity involving ASL proponents. Developed in the 1960's at Gallaudet University, Cued Speech showed substantial success in helping deaf children learn English, which led Gallaudet University in 1975 to embrace it as a solution to English illiteracy among the deaf and stepped up funding for the program.

Independent research evidence showed remarkable English skills of even *totally-deaf* children educated with the Cued Speech method, compared to those using sign or oral methods, which has led to increased usage worldwide.

However, culturally-deaf leaders have fought back with threats and intimidation. This included the burning of crosses on the lawns of Cued Speech supporters at Gallaudet.

In 1995, for whatever reasons not quite clear, the culturally-deaf dominated Gallaudet administration cancelled the Cued Speech program. [4-20]

Another interesting alternative to the current methods of educating the deaf child is home schooling. While obviously not for every parent, but for those who are capable, it merits serious consideration. A parent would have the flexibility to adjust methods to suit the needs of her deaf child rather than subject the child to an educational facility system which may be unsuited for some.

One *deaf* parent related her own experience teaching her (hearing) children, in a published report about home schooling. While it may be a journey for both the parent and the child, the rewards in the end appear richer. [4-21]

CHAPTER FIVE
GRIM REALITIES INSIDE A DEAF WORLD

NEW DISCLOSURES INDICATE GALLAUDET REVOLT PRECIPITATED BY OFF-CAMPUS ORCHESTRATORS
The so-called student revolt at Gallaudet University is often seen as a successful protest and considered by many to be justified. The revolt grew out of the university's decision to hire a hearing person to fill the vacant presidency.

However, recent disclosures have shed more light on what really happened during the revolt. It appears both the media and the general public have been manipulated into believing this was a *student protest*, when quite to the contrary, the protest was actually orchestrated by off-campus groups.

These new disclosures clearly indicate we must reevaluate our perception of what actually happened during the revolt and the final outcome.

These outside orchestrators who had nothing to lose were able to manipulate a few students into becoming involved using an *"end hearing oppression of the deaf"* pennant which provided an excuse to skip classes and midterms during a spring-like break in the weather. Few students actually supported the idea of a deaf president and it was difficult to even raise their interest.

Evidence shows some students were *forced* to participate by means of coercive methods which helped bolster the number of students appearing to be in revolt.

The group of non-students who orchestrated the protest were also involved in the selection of the student leaders who were to take their place. Two of the four eventual student leaders actually supported the *hearing* candidate in the beginning.

At one point, the non-student orchestrators contacted a TV station to report on a loosely organized sit-in, in which most participants were actually recruited to "stage" a demonstration for the media. With media attention, the demonstrators gave a performance which was then reported as mob behavior.

Deaf staff members at Gallaudet originally hesitated to get on the deaf president bandwagon. Only after the protest was well underway, and especially during a hastily called faculty meeting, did many reverse their stance. Witnesses described the meeting as a mob atmosphere, with threats and overwhelming pressure to support the students. Supporters of the hearing president were intimidated, shouted down and prevented from speaking.

Other deaf community leaders who had originally supported the hearing candidate for president, also succumbed to student pressure *after* the Gallaudet protest was well underway.

When a decision was made to select a hearing president, the university administration did not send a representative to announce the decision tactfully to the students. Many feel had this been done, or perhaps delayed a week until spring break, there would have been a peaceful outcome. Instead, the students heard an explanation from one of the non-student orchestrators, who gave an incomplete and not entirely correct explanation for the decision, which many of these angry people accepted as fact.

Newspapers and television disregarded crucial facts about the revolt. Illegal activities, coercion and the fact it was not started by students went unreported. In fact, the media portrayed the protest as being morally, legally and ethically correct.

The media also downplayed comments by the leaders of the protest frequently referring to the "plantation mentality" of many hearing people. Many feel had this been reported, some public support for the protesters might have waned.

Interpreters also had a hand in the ultimate outcome of the protest. Since most media access to the protesters went through them, mis-interpretation (although perhaps not deliberately) fueled the rage of the students who were given misinformation, and *pro-student* embellishments were added to the students' responses by some interpreters during media questionings.

During the height of the protest, a selection committee member speaking to a crowd of protesters was unaware an interpreter had difficulty interpreting her comments and the hostile crowd saw a non-flattering comment about deaf people which was quite contrary to what she actually said. This inflamed the protesters and she was never given an opportunity to correct the interpreter's error. The rage which followed resulted in the burning of her effigy and her erroneously insulting statements were published and are still repeated to this day.

NO DIGNITY FOR JOSHUA

The Gallaudet revolt was viewed by some at the time as bypassing the political process, prompting a network commentator to mention "something approaching anarchy," after he attempted to seek solutions for a compromise between the two sides appearing on his show.

As a major university nearly entirely dependent on federal funding (78.5 *million* dollars per year as of 1994), all taxpayers have a right to know the truth. 5-1

Did the end justify the means? To be sure, new public awareness helped all kinds of deaf people across the board. Doors were opened, the ADA sailed through. The deaf squeaky wheel was greased.

But at what cost? The public succumbed to anarchy. The media were manipulated. We saw the rise of the militant deaf, and a new unrealistic cavalier attitude among many Gallaudet students. This question will be ultimately answered by historians.

In the aftermath, years later, a deaf studies student and activist summed up the feeling of many: I supported a deaf president but did not approve of the approach. And now, anyone from Gallaudet has a real attitude problem, and is not in touch with reality in the real world. They will have no part of hearing people and that I do not like.

THE AMERICANS WITH DISABILITIES ACT

A deaf man made these observations: 'We have come a long way. Deaf people were once ostracized or stoned. St. Augustine declared us uneducable. But today, with the help of the Americans with Disabilities Act (ADA), our playing field has been leveled. But perhaps we have gone overboard, to where now it is fashionable to complain of discrimination, real or imagined.' As a result of this, we are seeing a rise of anti-

ADA activity and a Congressional review of the ADA is possible. Frivolous lawsuits filed by the deaf and other disabled people may prove to be the undoing of the ADA. 5-2

Asking for a little common sense, a culturally-deaf newspaper noted how some deaf people's trivial demands for ADA compliance make all deaf people look bad, not to mention making a mockery of the ADA.

For example, a deaf woman *sued* a fire department after her application to be a fire fighter was denied! Exactly how was she to communicate under emergency situations holding a fire hose? What about cries for help? Was an interpreter to be with her at all times?

In a case of literally barking up the wrong tree, many culturally-deaf individuals are spending enormous time ensuring accessibility of their hearing-ear dogs, when there are far more serious issues in dire need of attention.

Obviously hearing-ear dogs should be granted access to most facilities used by deaf people, but to *sue* a fast food chain because they were once denied access? How is a hearing-ear dog going to aid a deaf person in a fast food restaurant? I wonder how many deaf people are waiting for the outcome of these lawsuits so they can bring their dogs into McDairy King? Even some culturally-deaf leaders agree this is frivolous. 5-3

Trivial ADA claims are not unique to just members of the deaf community. Observers have outlined how disabled people, while requesting more disability benefits *and getting them*, turn around and bite the hand that feeds them. They say current conditions are the best ever for disabled people, yet many have become 'downright unappeasable.' 5-4

NO DIGNITY FOR JOSHUA

As a slap in the face to many deaf leaders who helped convince Congress to enact the ADA, there have been several reports of deaf individuals stealing equipment many businesses are now required by law to provide. Unavailability of TTY's at hotels, for example, is popping up because a previous deaf visitor stole it.

The general public is becoming aware and fed up with these trivial claims. In fact, recent data show the great majority of ADA claims are without merit and only thirteen percent of ADA decisions are found in favor of the claimant.

In one landmark court decision regarding the ADA, a jury ruled a disgrunted deaf patient was *not* discriminated against by her doctor in not providing an interpreter. The doctor was able to prove the patient was able to *communicate effectively* in previous visits and there was no real medical urgency at the time. The jury believed this was a well-educated woman who could read and write, and therefore communication was not compromised. This may be a harbinger of things to come as disabled people lose more public sympathy. [5-5]

We all need to be careful we do not become consumed by overzealous trivial claims, or the ADA may disappear as fast as it came on the horizon.

SOCIAL SECURITY DISABILITY BENEFITS

Long overdue changes have been proposed for Social Security disability benefits, of which one will find a great many recipients in the deaf community, including upwards of 70 to 80% of residential deaf school graduates. Supplemental Security Income (SSI) would no longer be an entitlement benefit, thus the loss of a safety net for the deaf. In addition, the Social Security Administration has resumed aggressive

NO DIGNITY FOR JOSHUA

reviewing of all 1.4 million disability entitlement benefit (SSD) recipients. The SSD program is often considered an "obstacle" to employment for many disabled people. It is hoped these new strategies make it easier for disabled to make the switch to employment. 5-6

Many of us feel *all* deaf recipients should be eventually eased off this dependency. After all, so many other government funds support the deaf, including a deaf university, so one must ask why continue the support?

One of the biggest problems with Social Security in the deaf community is it has an unseemly reputation of being a "prestige benefit," perfectly acceptable and even desirable.

An example of this: One time I ran across someone I had not seen for nearly a decade. After exchanging pleasantries, I asked him what he had been doing (with his life). While not totally surprised with his response, I detected an inappropriate sense of pride when he proclaimed "(I get) $999 a month from Social Security." After 10 years out of school, it was the greatest accomplishment in his life he felt he had to share with me.

Many of these culturally-deaf people will *never* get off the handout rolls but they will spend a great deal of time talking about their fun and engaging lifestyles, some with new homes and vehicles, complete with future plans for travelling and social functions, all at taxpayer expense.

At a minimum, Social Security must be replaced with a more socially unacceptable *handout* so labeled to discourage some culturally-deaf people from planning a lifestyle around it.

Everybody in the deaf community knows of members who supplement their Social Security benefits by working "under the table."

NO DIGNITY FOR JOSHUA

One entrepreneurial deaf business owner employed many of these recipients and paid them less than minimum wage. Not only was he able to underbid his hearing competitors for contracts, he was able to build his bank account for a luxurious retirement at an early age, at which time he also started receiving Social Security disability benefits himself, as he no longer had a job!

This just goes to show how some culturally-deaf have made a mockery out of the Social Security program and the taxpayers who fund it.

EMPLOYMENT AND THE CULTURALLY DEAF

Deaf leaders and educators are recognizing that too many culturally-deaf people are unprepared to enter the job market. Experts say they usually have fourth grade reading levels and most cannot even read newspapers. Employers are saying the inability to communicate is the main reason deaf people are not hired.

Many staff members at Gallaudet are concerned that a 'sheltered, and academically undemanding' atmosphere there is leaving deaf students unprepared for jobs in the mainstream society. In fact, over time, Gallaudet has received a number of letters from governmental agencies and private businesses indicating they can no longer hire Gallaudet graduates because they simply cannot read and write.

Many teachers are claiming they cannot spend the extra time to prepare students for employment, as it is 'not our problem what happens after they leave the school.' They say they must only ensure students get higher scores which indicate that teachers are doing their jobs. 5-7

In a recent rehabilitation self-assessment survey, the deaf were shown to have the lowest percentage with employment, lowest of family income and lowest in education among all disabled people. This clearly indicates many past and current methods of educating the deaf are somewhat ineffective. 5-8

At this writing, there is an emotional public debate among deaf educators, triggered by a prominent orally-educated writer's article in a major newspaper. This debate has engulfed just about everybody, but what seems to be promising here is that for the first time, the *employability* of deaf individuals is the focus. 5-9

With all this new public scrutiny, these outcries and debates may lead to new approaches in educating the deaf. If everybody can set aside their bitterness, perhaps this is a blessing in disguise.

In recent years, another barrier has been inadvertently placed in front of culturally-deaf job applicants.

Many employers are giving pre-employment "ethical screening tests," which may confuse deaf applicants unfamiliar with the purpose. Repetitive questions in a slightly different form are often asked to see if the applicant gives the same answer, as an honesty check. Screenings of these kinds are questionable in the first place, but unfortunately many employers use them to weed out the undesirable, inadvertently eliminating many deaf job applicants. Perhaps a few well chosen lawsuits may discontinue the practice entirely. (Deaf legal beagles-take note.) 5-10

INTERPRETERS, A LOVE-HATE RELATIONSHIP
Many culturally-deaf people have a love-hate relationship with sign language interpreters. They are often viewed by some deaf people as a necessary evil.

NO DIGNITY FOR JOSHUA

In the midst of this interpreter-deaf power struggle, interpreter advocates are asking for deaf leaders and interpreters to work together and resolve the growing mutual hatred. Concerns of interpreters 'not being welcome in the deaf community' and the misconception of 'living off the deaf' must be dealt with. The bottom line for interpreters is to earn enough to make a living or they will have to find another profession.

While some movement on both sides to try to resolve their differences is underway, progress is being hindered with a preliminary proposal by a prominent culturally-deaf organization to regulate interpreter fees and to put a "cap" on the fees charged by free-lance interpreters.

Such actions may be illegal and impossible to enforce. Worst of all, it will drive many good interpreters out of the business. Basically we are talking about the law of supply and demand. You get only what you pay for. Free competitive market conditions will resolve these problems, not more rules and regulations. The deaf need to be reminded they do not "own" sign language or interpreters. Ideas to attract more people into becoming interpreters are sorely needed.

For deaf people, this interpreter shortage is critical to the point where they sometimes cannot even find interpreters for funerals, adding to the emotional turmoil.

Interpreter advocates say job opportunities and financial rewards are great, but warned one should not get involved just because of feeling sorry for the deaf. 5-11

On the down side, interpreters face a rise of repetitive-stress injuries (carpal tunnel syndrome). In fact, school districts are finding a large percentage of the staff interpreters have these problems. This can cause some to leave the profession.

Leaders of the deaf community should keep this in mind as they consider future interpreter standards. 5-12

DEADLY ONLY IN OUR TIMES

The rising problem of gang violence has victimized innocent deaf bystanders who happened to be conversing in sign language and making a sign similar to a gang's "namesign."

Several letters of the deaf manual alphabet closely resemble gang members' namesigns (such as "V" and "L") which they often use to identify friend or foe.

There have been several instances when deaf people have been severely injured for inadvertently displaying a rival gang namesign. These provoked and angry gang members may not have known these persons were deaf.

CENSORSHIP WITHIN THE DEAF COMMUNITY, BIG BROTHER REALLY IS WATCHING

1984 came and went, but traces of George Orwell's classic tale exist in the deaf community today. Not only has reference to this been made by other writers, it is a chilling revelation to note the similarities in how militant deaf leaders are telling deaf people what to say, read, and especially, think.

One example: A columnist for a large culturally-deaf newspaper suggested perhaps some of us were "out of bounds" for taking up the task of writing deaf-related books. He was implying such undertakings should only be left up to culturally-deaf leaders and "experts," such as himself, who believe *only they* know what is best for *all* deaf people.

While obviously book critics can say anything they want, I bring this issue up to point out how far militants will go in their attempt to shield the mainstream society from unflattering truth about the deaf community. Information targeted to parents of deaf children is a primary concern for these militants.

Our free speech rights are guaranteed to everyone by the U.S. Constitution and the Bill of Rights. These institutions have no meaning to many militant deaf leaders. Numerous deaf community insiders can attest to harassment, intimidation and threats for having spoken out. Many others are held hostage, disagreeing with leadership, but afraid to speak and face the wrath of the deaf militants.

In one case, in an attempt to keep some revealing information from reaching the general public, a culturally-deaf professor engaged in blatant censorship by using his esteemed position with his university to *threaten* the publishing company's reputation should a certain book be released. Intervention by lawyers circumvented that activity.

This is especially disturbing when one considers the far-reaching consequences of eminent leaders advocating censorship and book banning. Further, he insults his colleagues at other major schools and universities, deaf centers, and deaf publications who have strongly endorsed and *welcomed* the publication of this information.

In this case, our free society prevailed when the requisitioning librarian at this professor's university deemed the book worthy enough, after reviewing testimonial information, to purchase and add to the university library collection.

In another case at a national convention for a culturally-deaf organization, one culturally-deaf leader was outraged that a certain book was being sold by independent deaf vendors who purchased space in the exhibition hall. He delivered a tirade including making a comparison to extremist counter-cultural terrorists groups.

The book in question was written by a culturally-deaf writer and published and distributed by privately-owned and deaf-owned businesses. It was also highly recommended by many esteemed deaf individuals and a number of convention attendees were interested enough after examination to purchase a copy of this book.

Some of us had thought this leader was truly concerned for the future of deaf children only to witness him tarnish his reputation with this censorship activity.

Some deaf militants have succeeded in convincing a number of publicly funded deaf resource centers to remove or prevent public access to certain material which may be in conflict with deaf culture ideology. Most of these service centers are supposed to be bias-free resource centers. Such centers can easily be held accountable by reporting this censorship to the governmental or non-profit agencies typically funding their existence.

Deaf censorship also occurs in Canada. To the surprise of many Americans, news blackouts and publication bans are common in Canada as many feel the trade-off is worth it to prevent the rise of problems with pornography and violence. In the United States, this freedom is absolute which explains why it is difficult to ban even truly offensive material.

While there is movement in Canada of free-speech groups trying to correct this, many Canadians drive across the border for access to full information not available at home. 5-13

Unfortunately for the Canadian deaf, one militant leader misused the intent of Canadian law to prevent what he perceived as non-flattering information about the deaf community from being exposed. His scare tactics may have worked on the uninformed, but certainly raised the eyebrows of his colleagues.

He has also apparently informed other Canadian culturally-deaf leaders of how they can utilize this "misinterpretation" to shut down information not to their liking. I wonder how many deaf Canadian citizens are in the dark because of activity like this?

One publisher gets right to the point: "When a decision is made for political reasons to deliberately prevent readers from choosing a certain book, what is it but blatant censorship? It is a chilling experience to come face to face with the Thought Police." [5-14]

GALLAUDET UNIVERSITY: A LONG HISTORY OF DECEPTION

Some are raising questions about Gallaudet's dubious history and believe the university administration still is not being honest with the general public, and especially our elected officials today.

Evidence shows Gallaudet forefathers and later administrations used mistruths, deceptive practices, cover-ups and manipulation of public officials starting in the 19th century as a means of obtaining funding and legitimacy. While some of this may have been in reaction to the "oppression of the deaf" at that time, many fear some of these techniques and traditions are still used today.

One example: Gallaudet recently was ranked 2nd in a national magazine for "best value" for colleges and universities in the northern part of the United States. The current administration quickly proclaimed 'pride in offering the best program at a cost that does not sacrifice the quality of our programs' in response to the ranking. What the Gallaudet officials did not mention was the federal government subsidizes the nearly 70% difference between the actual cost to operate the university and the amount collected from the artificially low tuition fee which was the basis for the magazine's evaluation criteria. *None* of the other schools in the report had this advantage. The Gallaudet administration *should have publicly set the record straight* instead of claiming this false prestige they did not deserve.

Gallaudet is no "great value" to the U.S. taxpayers. Gallaudet is not a public institution and some are wondering why we are paying $78 million a year to an "independent-non profit" school? Many of the best and brightest deaf students are going to other esteemed deaf college programs (NTID and CSUN) at a cost substantially cheaper than at Gallaudet.

In fact, since the Rehabilitation Act of 1973 and the ADA in 1990, there has been no need for most of Gallaudet to continue to exist as all. Colleges and universities are now *required* to accommodate deaf students. In reality, the need for a college to cater exclusively to the deaf may exist only in the minds of the culturally-deaf leadership. One writer summed this up by stating how 'taxpayers are now spending $78 million a year for a very large and expensive social club.'

In the Spring of 1997, the Gallaudet University School of Education and Human Services will be reviewed for continued accreditation. A number of outraged deaf people are submitting testimony requesting accreditation not be renewed. They are using many of the arguments I have brought up in this and previous chapters, especially on the problems surrounding ASL-based education.

Others are pointing out 'how can a university with only 1,500 students but having 1,000 staff members rank so "abysmally" low in almost all academic standards rankings?'

Transcripts of students show "A" grades in English for graduates who can't even read and write, silent testimony to the sad state of affairs there. One has to wonder exactly *how* did Gallaudet become a *University?*

A deaf editor writes "obviously any 'University' whose graduates are only borderline literate is not deserving of the name" and reminds the accreditation board that "proficiency in ASL is not an alternative to literacy."

To underline the absurdity of all this, one report disclosed the president of Gallaudet is paid in excess of $200,000 per year, making him one of the highest paid of *all* university presidents. 5-15

OTHER DUBIOUS ACHIEVEMENTS

A well-known culturally-deaf activist brought the collective image of the deaf community to a new low during an incident which happened in Florida during emergency evacuation for an imminent hurricane.

After accidentally locking her keys in her car which was blocking the pumps at a gas station, she *demanded* an interpreter before she would co-operate with authorities. The police spent hours persuading her to allow her car to be moved out of the way (at the expense offered by the owner of the gas station) during this emergency. She steadfastly refused to co-operate until an interpreter was present.

Finally, after hindering attempts to move her car, creating a disturbance, a traffic tie-up, and making obscene gestures at the police and service station employees, the police reluctantly held her briefly while her car was moved to another place on the lot. Afterwards she said "they (the police) raped my mind." 5-16

An editor of a publicly funded deaf services center profiled two "successful and outstanding" deaf citizens in a cover story in the center's monthly magazine.

Completely left out was the fact *both* of them were long-term recipients of Social Security benefits. This was a slap in the face to many other deaf people in this area who had *actual jobs*. This service agency also sponsored a Social Security workshop with our tax dollars covering, among other things, how to apply. Refreshments were served too.

In reference to doctors who perform the Cochlear Implant surgery in deaf children, one prominent culturally-deaf leader was quoted as saying: "Like the Nazis, they seem to enjoy experimenting on little children." A dean at Gallaudet University and a past President of the National Association of the Deaf has said: "Hearing parents are not qualified to decide about implants." An author, professor and deaf sympathizer indicated in a published statement the cochlear implantation of a deaf child is a mistake similar to the past practice of doctors performing lobotomies. [5-17]

One culturally-deaf leader admitted he disrupted proceedings during a public deaf solution-seeking session, for media attention. When pressed about a limited number of supporters at this disruption, he implied that most (deaf people) 'don't know what to do,' and made reference to others (apparently those who agreed with the other deaf factions) as "brown-nosers." He had also claimed it was a 'known fact oral deaf people have higher mental health problems' but was unable to back this up when asked about it later. [5-18]

A major award-winning television program recently produced by the culturally-deaf, covering events related to the

Gallaudet student revolt, contained major factual inaccuracies. There was no mention of the non-student orchestrators who actually started the revolt. Even a rally held at the U.S. Capitol, celebrating five years since the student protest, repeated factual inaccuracies. 5-19

Deaf gate crashers ruined what was touted as a highly successful "ASL Festival," a major event in the deaf community. The deaf promoters admit the primary cause for the substantial deficit for this event showcasing ASL and deaf culture, was these non-paying attendees. This forced the deaf organizers to seek help outside the deaf community to bail them out of financial default. 5-20

One culturally-deaf leader said publicly that sending a 4-year-old child to residential deaf school away from (hearing) parents, *is "wonderful"* for the deaf. 5-21

Some have described how certain culturally-deaf leaders have held public forums with unseemly topics such as: "Who owns the deaf child?" In this case culturally-deaf leaders feel hearing parents are obligated to 'give up their deaf child' to the deaf community. 5-22

A pro-ASL linguistics policy at Gallaudet University, which had the support of many culturally-deaf people, backfired when implementation was attempted.

This extreme linguistic policy required signing ASL in all areas of the school. For example, a hearing teacher talking to non-signing hearing visitors (with no deaf people present) was *required* to sign to them in ASL, then let an interpreter voice the hearing teacher's signs.

The university president ultimately rescinded the policy after a backlash from parents, members of Congress, and other esteemed deaf people. In the aftermath, a dean (a proponent of the policy) was re-assigned, and the president faced the wrath of the culturally-deaf for pulling the plug. 5-19

Gallaudet University officials set up an English Literacy project to help counter the finding that seventy percent of the undergraduates have difficulty reading college level textbooks. Deaf militants have fought back claiming a conspiracy to get rid of their native language and oppress the deaf.

Another new twist to this: Rather than trying to improve their English, some Gallaudet students are demanding the staff provide exams using ASL instead of English. 5-23

And finally, four self-described outspoken supporters of ASL and deaf culture are suing Gallaudet University after they, along with many others, were laid-off due to federal budget cutbacks. These un-tenured instructors are angry because they believe they are being singled out for their outspokenness and are asking compensation of *ten million* of your and my taxpayer dollars! 5-24

CHAPTER SIX
COCHLEAR IMPLANTS IN YOUNG DEAF CHILDREN

ORWELLIAN FANTASY

Someone wrote of what could be an Orwellian fantasy in describing a future viewed by many culturally-deaf leaders. 'Imagine having a deaf child and going to doctors to find out if there is a cure, only to be told successful procedures were once commonplace, but were discontinued because curing deafness is *wrong*.'

This writer is not being far-fetched. If these culturally-deaf leaders could have their way, this would become a reality. The motives of these leaders became public knowledge when a prime-time television news magazine aired a story on Cochlear Implants (or CI). They bitterly opposed the Food and Drug Administration`s (FDA) approval of the device as well as attacking the network for airing the story. "Child abuse" and "genocide" are words culturally-deaf leaders are using to characterize these implants.

The writer is pointing out parents of deaf children are being 'castigated for not allowing their kids to be deaf,' and doctors are 'finding their work compared to that of Nazi doctors.' In the midst of all this, deaf children are puzzled why some people think it is 'bad to hear.' 6-1

CONTRADICTIONS AND LIES

It has been suggested words like "ethnic purification" and "cultural genocide" from militant deaf leaders are used to attract media attention. These leaders insist CI's do not work, yet at the same time say they work so well, it is genocide. Contradictions like these, as well as inane comments such as declaring doctors unethical and referring to the CI as "The Final Solution," are causing many to be confused and angry and sometimes even lead to violence. 6-2

Militants spreading misinformation about the CI has resulted in mass confusion, even among many educated deaf people. Typical confusion about the CI ran along the lines of: 'I don't know much about the implant, but I'm against it...some have died from it, others got brain damage.' None of these statements is true, but is believed by many in the deaf community. 6-3

Other false and misleading statements from culturally-deaf leaders being foisted on the public include "It is brutal to open a child's skull ... just to rob that child of a birthright of silence," as well as "There is absolutely no question that our government has a hidden agenda for deaf children much akin to Nazi experiments on Holocaust victims." 6-4

The World Federation of the Deaf (WFD) says the CI operation is *unethical* because we do not know beforehand if the child will benefit. In addition, the president of the WFD spread misinformation when he wrote, among other things, how several deaf individuals *died* from the implant. None of these statements is true and all are quite contrary to the facts.

The facts are: Hundreds of scientific research results have been published over the course of a decade noting the successes with the CI. In addition, it appears surgical complications are rare and the device itself not a hazard. [6-5]

It is important to point out that while the National Association of the Deaf (NAD) has a number of committees (such as the ADA and Law sections) which advocate progress for all deaf people, nevertheless one committee exists only for the purpose of *opposing* implants for deaf children.

Culturally-deaf leaders speak of 'a needless pain and torture' a child endures with the surgery and want to prevent any new developments. They have stated, 'there is no evidence of material benefit, ...enhancement of speech, or English...' despite hundreds of published reports stating otherwise.

Until recently, little was said publicly by organizations such as the NAD about the loss of a culture these medical advancements led to, but now this is the underlying reason for opposition to any medical treatment of deafness.

These positions weakened the NAD's credibility as an advocacy group for most deaf people, and one now has to conclude the NAD is biased toward serving only a select few.

Sympathizers with the deaf community have argued CI technology does not benefit the deaf community and therefore is unethical. If this argument be valid, then medical efforts to eradicate Rubella and Cytomegalovirus, both leading causes of deafness, must also be "unethical."

At any rate, it is quite obvious, as a prominent hearing specialist pointed out, the true "target" of some culturally-deaf leaders is "*any method of treatment or prevention of deafness that is effective,*" not just the CI. Further, some have noted that opponents of the CI who utilize untruths and misinformation to achieve their agendas violate ethical standards of truthfulness and actually may be hindering those whom they claim to be helping. 6-6

DEAFNESS: IS IT A DISABILITY OR A CULTURE?

Culturally-deaf leaders believe deafness is *not* a disability but rather a *culture*, never mind the billions they reap yearly from numerous disability-related benefits.

Some believe since these leaders feel deafness is not a disability, then they should not be covered by the protection of the ADA and deafness-related discrimination claims are ineligible. In addition, they would not be eligible for *any* disability entitlement benefits such as Social Security. These culturally-deaf leaders insist they are still eligible for all disability-related benefits. 6-7

Logically, both arguments cannot possibly be valid. Those in the hearing professions say that this continuing support of both sides of the argument by colleagues in the deaf community is disappointing. 6-6

Questions are now being raised that perhaps those in the deaf community *should* give up their billions if they are convinced they are not really disabled.

Many of us hope more people pin these militants down to choosing either a disability or a culture. Having let militant deaf leaders have it both ways all these years may explain the mess we are in today. By making culturally-deaf leaders live with the consequences of decisions they make, we can expect rational behavior in the future.

As for the rest of us, one doctor summed it up perfectly, hitting the nail squarely on the head, when he stated: 'When I look into a child's cochlea and see damaged hair cell endings, I do not see a culture.' 6-8

HOW WELL DO THEY WORK?

Decades of extensive research and hundreds of published reports convinced the FDA to approve the implant in the first place. They have also continued to approve more and more devices. [6-6]

Recently, major universities doing research into CI recipients confirmed significant benefits to the users of these implants, especially in speech development and speech discrimination. They conclude the implant is beneficial to auditory development in young deaf children.

Key sources say most implanted deaf children, including those "born deaf," are able to hear and understand.

The National Institute of Health recently called for expanded use of the CI. As of 1996, 15,000 adults and children have the CI and it is believed to be able to help one million other deaf individuals. The NIH say the safety record is very good and experts feel more people will now opt for it. [6-9]

MEANWHILE, INSIDE THE DEAF COMMUNITY...

CI recipients are referred to as *CI survivors* inside the deaf community and are often bullied for not accepting their deafness. Leaders of the deaf community claim these people face more discrimination than non-CI deaf people, but ironically, most of that discrimination comes from within the deaf community. [6-10]

CI recipients will never be really accepted into the deaf community in spite of the fact they can reverse an eventual population decline in the deaf community itself.

Culturally-deaf leaders are concerned CI proponents do not consider them when making CI decisions, but let us not forget, it works both ways. Many culturally-deaf leaders do not care about new medical advances. This could be considered a form of reverse-oppression to some deaf people in the community who would like to know of these advances.

In recent years, culturally-deaf leaders have been invited to participate in many public forums regarding decisions and public policies about the CI, but often these leaders do not take full advantage of those opportunities.

In one case, the deaf community was invited to a public hearing to consider funding of a CI program but they declined to attend. When the decision did not go their way, they erupted in outrage. 6-10

In another case, an opportunity to convince CI proponents of their concerns was blown by the deaf community representatives. Invited to a symposium to present their views on CI's for children, they weakened their credibility with the attendees when it was obvious during their presentation they did not attend any of the other speakers' sessions.

Among other things, they argued for more research and smaller study groups, seemingly unaware the CI field is decades beyond that stage. 6-11

Leaders of the deaf community have also been using the high cost of CI's as an argument against the device. They claim greedy doctors are only interested in the money CI's generate.

This has some of us wondering since when has anyone in the deaf community been concerned about high costs for anything? They are certainly not concerned about the high cost many members of the deaf community burden our society with. They certainly are not being asked to pay for the CI. The fact is: Many CI centers lose money and rely on outside support to maintain their programs. 6-12

Culturally-deaf leaders have pointed out that in some residential schools one may find a few CI recipients who have not seemed to benefit from the device, singling them out as typical CI recipients, disregarding the fact that the lack of necessary auditory training, reinforcement and monitoring makes the schools themselves the *cause* of failure, not merely witness to it. [6-13]

One must remember that for the average child with the device, the residential deaf school is not the best choice of an educational placement. It would appear the more successful the CI user is, the less likely he would end up at a residential deaf school.

Some within the deaf community believe defeat is on the horizon. One was quoted as saying "...once the implants are perfected, it'll be a lost battle (trying to preserve deaf culture)."

In reality, it was a battle only in the minds of militant deaf leaders. Most of us were just interested in preserving choices for parents of deaf children. [6-14]

LOOKING BEYOND MILITANT RHETORIC

A number of people have concluded it is clear the motive behind the culturally-deaf leaders' opposition to the CI is the fact a large percentage of the deaf community will cease to exist. "...the future of the deaf community is at stake. An entire sub-culture of America will no longer exist." a professor at Gallaudet said. [6-3]

A deaf editor of a deaf-related periodical recently spoke out: "(deaf radicals believe) that deafness is not a disability at all, and that it is wrong to try to prevent, cure or treat it." and "their most vehement stance of all is their opposition to the use of CI's." He also says: "Their claim of deafness not being a disability amounts to hypocrisy when the truth is they wish to prevent extinction of 'deaf culture'." 6-15

A number of people are fearful of culturally-deaf leaders obtaining control of deaf children ahead of (hearing) parental rights. These militants are actively taking steps to convince mainstream leaders to defer all decisions regarding deaf children to the leaders of the deaf community. This especially includes any decision regarding the CI.

Fortunately, our courts have continued to rule culturally-deaf leaders *cannot* intrude on the rights of parents to choose what they feel is best for their child. 6-16

At the risk of repeating myself, many of us encourage action be taken to have culturally-deaf leaders held accountable for their actions. In the long run, historians and scholars will see beyond the rhetoric of the militant deaf, but now is the only time we can do something for our deaf children of today.

Many of us are quite bothered when we see the substantial amount of the time of these medical professionals being devoted to dealing with militants and other leaders of the culturally-deaf.

There are a quite a number of us anxiously awaiting the next new medical development which could eventually benefit us. But instead, time is being wasted fighting politically with individuals who *don't* want to be helped.

Another real concern is medical professionals with a distaste for politics may be driven to other fields.

Finally, I must stress that deaf individuals or parents of a deaf child should not make a final decision regarding the CI on the basis of reading this writer's research. I hope to have provided insight into what is going on on both sides of the table to help the reader understand the issues under fire. Only those working with the CI in the medical profession are able to determine whether you or your deaf child can benefit from the implant.

GENETIC MEDICINE

We are at the point in history where it is now time to discuss whether disabilities or even things considered characteristics, such as baldness, short stature, and for some in the deaf community, deafness, will need to be changed to *preventable defects or diseases* with the advancement of genetic medicine. Some are asking whether it may even be irresponsible in the future to bear children without a thorough genetic physical, then if needed, genetic therapy to correct any defects. [6-17]

Technology already exists for a prenatal test to screen for the defective gene causing seventy percent of the cases of people of very short stature. Upon discovery of such genetic defects, parents can choose to terminate the pregnancy and try again later for another, healthier child.

While most deafness-related genes have yet to be identified, doctors say they are very close. This feared day of reckoning for culturally-deaf leaders is closer than they think, as recently scientists have discovered the mutated gene causing the most common type of deaf-blindness. (Usher's Syndrome) With the continuing advancement of genetic medicine, the ability to identify, correct or suppress a deafness-related defective gene may be as soon as tomorrow. [6-18]

This will open an ethical can of worms. The culturally-deaf are sure to argue deafness is an "alternative style of wellness." Questions will be raised: Is a defective gene a culture? Do doctors only repair genes which do not constitute a "culture?"

At any rate, if we allow genetic medicine to become ethically acceptable in our society, we cannot make exceptions to the rule. Who wants to explain to a deaf child the reason he or she is still disabled is because family elders in past generations deemed it important to "preserve" some specimen of an ancient "culture?"

It is interesting to note some people who are of short stature are speaking out against aborting fetuses found to have the defective gene. They have used very much the same argument many deaf leaders are using. But then, they are calling for the decision to be left up to parental discretion rather creating rules and regulations as we see happening in the deaf community.

Many deaf couples have already been requesting in health clinics wanting only deaf children. Discussions in the deaf community say it should work both ways: Pre-natal screening should allow deaf parents to abort a hearing fetus for those who desire deaf children. [6-19]

CHAPTER SEVEN
HEARING INJUSTICES

While hearing injustices to the deaf have been well-documented for more than a century now, I have often been asked to describe some of these injustices still occurring today. I offer some of my own personal experiences as well as a few publicly disclosed by others.

EMPLOYERS

While I was working for a past employer, management found it convenient to change work assignments for the employees by paging them to the manager's office. This of course put me at a disadvantage. I started losing out on choice assignments when my supervisors would simply bypass me rather than take the time to go look for me. Not wanting to fall into the trap of doing all the "grunt" work, I looked for a solution.

Bringing the subject up with company management normally should resolve this. However at this employer, there was a parade of supervisors over the years, many who were quite stressed out with other concerns.

I decided to work out an arrangement with a co-worker. He would tell me when *anybody* was paged. I would then just show up in the manger's office saying: "Is it my turn?"

or "I thought it was for me." Very often out of guilt, I would get the assignment anyway and, looking back, I probably ended up getting more choice assignments than I would have if I had normal hearing.

On another occasion we were introduced to yet another new supervisor. Fresh out of retail stores they were placed at the distribution center to manage union warehousemen and truck drivers to see how they handle pressure, a check for store management potential.

This new supervisor immediately gave me a clearly obvious "I'm better than you because I do not have a disability" look, and I dreaded the next few weeks.

Sure enough, the very next day after I returned from my delivery run, my new supervisor came outside and asked me point blank: "Do you have a driver's license?" He then went on to say the DMV should *not* be giving driver's licenses to hearing impaired people!

I steered clear of this guy until eventually he was promoted into upper-level management, where I'm sure he continued to inflict misery on disabled employees as he climbed the management ladder until (hopefully) caught with a major ADA violation.

AUDIOLOGISTS

Unfortunately, as one would think such would not be the case, a number of audiologists have tarnished the profession.

My Vocational Rehabilitation counselor once sent me to a hearing center to be evaluated for new hearing aids. The audiologist there engaged in a rather lengthy conversation with me about my past history and hearing impairment. When it was revealed I had attended a residential deaf school, the conversation took an ugly turn. All of a sudden he became uninterested and started speaking to me in over-emphasized syllables, with exaggerated mouth movements.

Another audiologist a few years later did exactly the same thing, only he *quit talking to me entirely!* He began using hand gestures and pointing to convey what he wanted me to do afterwards. The fact we had conversed by voice with no difficulty for 15 minutes prior to mentioning the words "deaf school" meant nothing.

The integrity of the profession was saved however by yet another audiologist who this time took genuine interest in my case. She mentioned how she had never met someone who had such a severe hearing loss combined with having attended a state residential deaf school and yet still able to speak and listen without too much difficulty.

In her investigation of "what went right" for me, she came to the conclusion that daily use of hearing aids, along with the early "mainstreaming" at a regular public school, might have made all the difference for me.

She commented on the large number of former state residential deaf school students she had worked with, who had a lesser degree of hearing loss, yet had no ability to understand speech and to speak.

MEDICAL PROFESSIONALS

While I have great respect for those in the field of medicine, a few of them have tarnished the profession. Many of us know of an arrogant doctor or nurse who has treated us in a non-dignified manner.

In a personal experience, during an evaluation for a new hearing aid at an ear specialist's clinic, I found the true meaning of indignation.

Knowing beforehand I was educated at a facility using a "signing" method, which was (soon to be obvious) against his ideology, during the examination this physician dished out the worst sort of disrespect for a human being I will not bother to get into.

To sum it up, he did not want anything to do with me. However, because of a contract with the state, he was obligated to accept all Vocational Rehabilitation clients. His attitude was memorable enough to recall decades later as this book was being put together.

An elderly deaf woman told of a terrifying incident occurring after she underwent a supposedly routine cataract operation on one eye. During the middle of the surgery, the eye surgeon realized he was in over his head and the deaf patient needed to be immediately transported to another hospital that had an advanced eye research center, and have a specialist continue the operation. The deaf woman remained anaesthetized during the whole process and was unaware what had transpired.

After the surgery, she was bandaged over *both* eyes, and was physically restrained for a week.

When she awoke, she could not move and could not see. She started screaming in panic and doctors gave her heavy medication to calm her down. Each time it wore off, they had to administer more medication as she resumed screaming.

Towards the end of the week, a team of doctors were trying to figure out what had occurred during the operation to cause this kind of response from the patient. The possibility of brain damage was seriously discussed.

When the bandages were finally removed, the doctors discovered what the problem was. The woman was deaf. *Nobody* there knew she was deaf. The woman's personal doctor failed to inform the other hospital staff of that fact. Nobody bothered to check with her husband at home (bedridden at the time) for information and he was supposedly assured by the first surgeon she was fine.

The woman endured a week in a dark medical-hell having no idea of what and why this was happening to her.

PUBLIC PLACES

One such incident began shortly after a deaf man met a friend in a restaurant. The deaf man began signing excitedly about an upcoming family event. The friend got engaged in sharing exciting news and they both continued signing about it for a few minutes.

Abruptly, a woman stood up from a table in the restaurant and said she had seen enough of this signing *bull-sh**!* And then she sought out the manager to put a stop to this conversation. To add further insult, the manager agreed with the hearing woman and ordered the deaf people to sign outside of the restaurant.

A hearing adult, the son of culturally-deaf parents, once pretended he was deaf in an upscale restaurant by using sign language. He and his date were stunned to overhear the restaurant staff refer to them as *idiots.*

In another case, an employee, after asking a deaf customer if he needed help and upon discovering he was deaf, muttered: "Well... I can't help you."

Prior to giving a live performance in a public facility, an internationally renowned actor ordered the deaf people and their interpreters to sit in the last row. Among other words used in his tirade against having interpreters for the deaf people were "ludicrous" and "ridiculous." The interpreters suggested to the deaf people they simply just walk out of the performance as this actor was undeserving of their presence. 7-1

NO DIGNITY FOR JOSHUA

A deaf friend with a window-facing office on the ground floor on a busy street is able to engage in sign language conversation with passersby through the window.

To people in the street, it sometimes appears as if a deaf person is signing to the building all by himself. My friend working inside the building wasn't easily seen unless you were standing right in front of the window.

While it was not uncommon to draw curious stares from passersby, it was not until one day a hearing sign language interpreter stopped at the window and signed to my friend. It became apparent some of these passersby were saying really nasty things to these supposedly deaf people.

In that particular case someone said *"you dumb sh**!"* The hearing interpreter who was signing turned around and immediately gave this person a public scolding!

A deaf nurse and social worker has come up with an interesting term, *deaf-phobia*, to describe bizarre actions by certain hearing people when encountering a deaf person. Nearly all deaf people run across one of these sooner or later.

She described how a deaf person once confronted a co-worker who habitually avoided him. In reaction to the confrontation, the hearing person yelled "GO AWAY" and protected herself by putting her hands up over her face.

The deaf person later found out the hearing co-worker was afraid by associating with him, she would become deaf herself. [7-2]

TELEPHONE RELAY SERVICE
The telephone relay service has been a tremendous boon for the deaf, hard-of-hearing and speech impaired. This is one of the best widely-available "equalizers" for the deaf,

allowing nearly unlimited and equal access to the telephone medium.

A deaf person calls a relay service operator by typing on a TTY (a keyboard-based telephone device for the deaf) and the relay operator in turn makes a simultaneous call to a regular "voice" number (a party without a TTY) and provides the voice for the deaf caller and vice-versa. In effect, a real-time conversation takes place between the deaf person and a hearing person on the telephone.

But interestingly enough, the greatest frustration in dealing with the relay service is not the technology, but the human factor.

Many in the mainstream society resist dealing with the relay service. Horror stories abound from nearly every deaf user of the relay service. Rude hang-ups and a lack of returned calls reveals an impatient society.

For instance, once I called a local retailer via the relay service to inquire about purchasing a thousand dollar item. As the relay operator tried to explain their function, the person I was calling interrupted and said: "This is a business line and we do *NOT* have time for this, "CLICK!" Obviously, my business went elsewhere, but not before calling them back and giving them a scolding.

Another time I left my phone number and relay number and instructions how to use the relay service with a repair facility to inform me when my vehicle was completed. After a few days, I called them to discover they had not even started because I "refused to answer the phone" when they called earlier about a minor item. They told me they did not have time to deal with the relay number and tried calling me direct.

One report told of using the relay service to order take-out food. After listening to the relay service explain their function, the restaurant employee muttered "Where do you live you little deaf-mute?"

Unfortunately, such behavior is quite common and it has been said the medical profession is the group most likely to object to calls received via relay. [7-3]

These few incidents just go to show the disabled have to overcome much more than their disability in our society.

WIRE AND WIRELESS COMMUNICATIONS

While telephone technology is rapidly advancing, deaf people are not always benefiting.

For example, there are technical drawbacks when relay calls are made and an automated answering system answers the call. Often, touch tone numbers need to be entered to complete the call. By the time the relay is made back to the deaf caller, the system may disconnect or put the deaf caller on an indefinite hold. The relay operator then has to repeat the process over and over before the call can get through. Many times we are asked to leave a message and again, before the deaf caller can reply, the answering system disconnects.

I will not even bother to get into how messages left on answering machines via relay service are almost never returned unless the person being called has *prior experience* with the relay service, and then only maybe.

A truly useful device for the deaf and hard-of-hearing is a FAX machine. But of course, everyone has to have one first. This device should eventually gain widespread use among deaf people as it is rather simple to use, economical and more personal than other modes of wire or wireless communication and a way to avoid using a relay service.

Deaf persons are able to send faxes without disclosure of their disability. This is a way to make that important "first impression," without first having to identify or explain a disability.

Email on computer on-line services provides the same thing. Usage among the deaf is growing. Deaf individuals with both FAX and Email capability can reach and communicate with the vast majority of businesses and services without ever identifying their deafness!

At this writing, cellular communications for the deaf are rather costly and not too convenient nor practical and usually both. For one thing, sound quality is very poor and cellular phones are mostly not compatible with hearing aids. TTY's, even portable ones, are somewhat bulky to carry, and one would still need to carry a cellular phone along with a connecting device and, of course, spare batteries for all three devices.

Cost is another prime concern as TTY calls take two to three times as long to conduct, even with the use of a relay service. There is currently no TTY discount for wireless use as there is for long distance calls placed with a wire phone.

Some deaf people have had success with pagers having digital readouts, and portable cellular fax machines. But by and large, economical, simple and convenient cellular phone service is still beyond reach for most of us.

Telephone and cellular providers have recently begun promoting cellular phones as necessary and prudent *personal security devices*. If they are going to seriously promote this notion, then they should be taking steps to ensure this personal security is available for the deaf.

Traditional access to police and public safety such as roadside emergency phones and pay phones, is being discontinued in with expectation of people using their cellular phones. For example, deaf people are insulted where highway signs used to describe future traffic information now only give a phone number to call.

Deaf leaders and legal beagles should take this opportunity to require development of a small and simple, one piece TTY/cellular device with a national cellular relay service, and usage fees billed at a reasonable rate. Let us not get left behind at the information *wayside*.

FUTURE TECHNOLOGY, DOES IT INCLUDE US?

Computer voice recognition technology is God-sent for many disabled people, offering hands-free interaction with computer devices. The added benefit of ease of use, and less repetitive stress injuries will accelerate this technology.

However, there is a *horrible* downside to this. With voice recognition, a computer keyboard and monitor is often no longer needed, leaving only the question of how are deaf people to use these devices? We certainly are not going to be able to hear or understand the computer-voiced prompts either.

In the future these keyboards and monitors may be eliminated from many devices, no longer being necessary for operation. Once manufacturers bring these cheaper keyboardless devices to market, competitors will soon follow or lose their market share. The deaf will have to buy expensive "dedicated" devices, if any are available at all!

Once again, we may find ourselves left behind unless deaf leaders unite and take steps *now* to ensure mass-produced goods of the future remain accessible and useful for hard-of-hearing or deaf people. 7-4

EPILOG

A FEW COMMENTS AND FINAL THOUGHTS...

There was once a tendency for hearing people to keep deaf people out of decision making on deaf issues. Deaf leaders have succeeded in reversing these conditions and now have a say in much of what happens in their lives. Unfortunately, militant deaf leaders have gotten carried away and are forcing their convictions on a majority of deaf people they clearly do not even represent.

Further, we are frankly quite tired of deaf militants using finger pointing and "hearing oppression" as an excuse for the problems with deaf education and maladies in the deaf community. We must no longer accept these excuses.

Many of us wish we were less discouraged about many aspects of the deaf community. We would like to ask these militant leaders, "Where is the justification for this behavior?" Moderation and cooperation will go a long way toward resolving the sad state of affairs many deaf people find themselves in today. The normalization of sexual abuse in the deaf community is just one example of misplaced priorities by culturally-deaf leaders.

We are *disabled* due to a human physical disfunction and things will never be made perfect for us. The rationale of disguising a disability as a culture will be difficult to explain to our perhaps needlessly deaf children of the future.

In the aftermath of the Gallaudet revolt an African-American deaf protester was asked if she was also involved with the black civil rights movement. "No," she said, "I'm too busy being deaf, but my hearing brother takes care of being black."

This is a stark reality check. Cultures are often a matter of perspective. A culture can quickly end when supplanted by a more immediate concern or begin when a lifestyle is threatened.

A common trend among many deaf militants is to attack the hearing researchers, as they claim these researchers do not know how to do research and are *always* wrong! Never mind that these deaf leaders do not often conduct parallel research to scientifically verify these supposed errors.

In a prime example, a notable culturally-deaf researcher quickly dismissed a recently published research paper that contains *irrefutable evidence* based on published statements by these *culturally-deaf leaders themselves,* clearly verifying their contradictions and mistruths. The deaf researcher implied it was not how things really are, even if the findings are technically correct.

Culturally-deaf leaders have destroyed their credibility among many by these mistruths, lies and contradictions. This has made it difficult for many of us to see things of redeeming value in the deaf community.

I (and certainly many of my readers) hope my next book will consist of more pleasant things to report.

REFERENCES
AND NOTES

Yerker Andersson, PhD., (1-94) *WFD News, (Do we want cochlear...)*
Jay Apperson, (2-95) *The Baltimore Sun (MD), (Deaf woman says...)*
Thomas Balkany, MD., Annelle V. Hodges, PhD., Kenneth W. Goodman, PhD., (1996) *Triological Society, (The ethics of Cochlear Implantation in young children)* University of Miami Ear Institute
Joan Beck, (1995) *Chicago Tribune (IL), (Use English as unifying force)*
Charles Berlin, PhD., (1996) *Sixth Symposium on Cochlear Implants in Children (Miami, FL),* Kresge Institute, New Orleans, LA
F. Berringer, (5-93) *New York Times, (Pride in a soundless world)*
Beverly Biderman, (Winter-94) *Contact, (A challenge for deaf culture)*
Arthur Caplan, PhD., (9-95) *Scientific American, (An improved future?)*
Paulette R. Caswell, JD., (1996-correspondence) AMICUS, Inc. Educational Services, Los Angeles, CA.
Prof. John B. Christiansen, Prof. Sharon N. Barnartt, (1995) *Deaf President Now!* Gallaudet University Press, Washington, DC
R. Coffey, (1992) *The Bicultural Center News, (Caitlin's story...)*
Noel Cohen, MD., (1996) *Sixth Symposium on Cochlear Implants in Children,* University of Miami (FL)
Noel Cohen, MD., (1994) *Am. Journal of Otology, (The ethics of CI...)*
Aly Colon, (3-96) *The Seattle Times (WA), (Sharing a boisterous silence)*
Roger O. Crockett, (8-96) *The Oregonian (OR), (Disabled discrimination claims climbs sharply)*
Dana D. De Mers, (4-96) *The Columbian (WA), (Technology may end 'deaf culture')*

NO DIGNITY FOR JOSHUA

Jennifer Dixon, (11-94) *Associated Press, (Welfare disaster ahead?)*

Frances Elton, (Winter-94) *Signpost, (Profile of Frances Elton)*, Int'l Sign Linguistics Assoc., University of Durham, England

Joan Emerick, RN, MSW., *Life After Deafness, (Dear social worker)*

Janet Filips, (2-94) *The Oregonian (OR), (A family crosses the sound barrier, Hearing the deaf)*,

Andrew Firth, (Various issues) *The NAD Broadcaster (MD)*

Josie Glausiusz, (1-96) *Discover, (The genes of 1995)*

Lew Golan, (1995) *Reading Between the Lips,* Chicago, IL. Bonus Books, Inc.

Lew Golan, (3-96) *The Washington Post (DC), (Dialogue of the deaf: What Gallaudet won't teach.)*

Ben Gose, (3-96) *The Chronicle of Higher Learning*

Laurence Hammack, (3-95) *Roanoke Times & World News (VA), (All deaf rape trial...)*

Dixie Imada, PhD., (10-95) *Life after Deafness, (A rose by any other...)*

Alexander C. Kafka, (9-94) *Newsday (Long Island, NY)*

Carol Kleiman, (9-95) *The Oregonian (OR), (Pros find personal, financial rewards in interpreting for the deaf)*

John F. Knutson, PhD., (1996-Correspondence)

John F. Knutson, PhD., Patricia M. Sullivan, PhD., (1993) *Topics in Language Disorders, (Comm. disorders as a risk factor in abuse)*

Ted Koppel, (3-88) *Nightline,* ABC News, New York, NY

Vanessa Kramer, (8-95) *Life After Deafness, (A home schooling...)*

Alice LaBarre, MA. (with excerpts from Florrie Burke), (11-93) *Hearing Health (TX), (Secrets, the sexual abuse of deaf children)*

Bertt Lependorf, (10-93) *The DCARA News (CA)*

Bertt Lependorf, (1-95) *Silent News (NY)*

Shawn Lovley, (Various issues) *The Community Ear (OR), (Lately...)*

Mike Males, (9-93) *In These Times,* Inst. for Public Affairs. Chicago, IL

Gayle McCullough, Otto J. Menzel, PhD, (1993) *Feud for Thought,* Life After Deafness, Bristol, VA

Otto J. Menzel, PhD., (1996-Correspondence)

Otto J. Menzel, PhD., (Various issues) *Life After Deafness (TN)*

Lori Mack, (1-95) *Small Press (Seattle, WA)*

Anita Manning, (5-96) *USA Today, (Gallaudet University is being sued)*

Hannah Merker, (10-95) *Life After Deafness, (Regarding...)*

Matthew S. Moore, (3-95) *Deaf Life (NY), (Publisher's note)*

NO DIGNITY FOR JOSHUA

Jim Oliver, (4-95) *Deaf Community News (WA)*
Mike Parker, (1996) *KEX Radio, (Sportsline)* Portland, OR
Prof. Frances M. Parsons, (1996-Correspondence)
Deborah Powell, (2-95) *British Deaf News,* Carlisle, Great Britain
M. Robinette, (2-93) *Seminars in Hearing*
Toni M. Rogers, (3-95) *Willamette Week (OR), (Painful signs),*
Robert A. Rosenblatt, (3-96) *LA Times-Washington Post Service,*
        (Disability recipients face scrutiny)
Ellen Roth, (12-93) *Deaf/HOH Newsletter (WA)*
Terry Ryther, (Various columns) *The Community Ear (OR)*
Paul Saevig, (2-94) *Life After Deafness, (A question for...)*
Debra J. Saunders, (Various columns) *The San Francisco Chronicle,*
        Creators Syndicate Inc.
Pete Schulberg, (3-95) *The Oregonian (OR), (CC beneficial...)*
Bobbie Beth Scoggins, (11-94) *The NAD Broadcaster (MD)*
Gil Shamir, (8-93) *Life After Deafness, (Deafness, not a disability?)*
A. Silver, (12-92), *TBC News, (Cochlear implant...)*
Birgitta Soderfeldt, 1994 *Signing in the Brain,* Uppsala University
Andrew Solomon, (8-94) *The New York Times, (Deaf is beautiful)*
Al Sonnenstrahl, (2-95) *Deaf Life (NY), (It is up to the hearing...)*
K. E. Strom, (2-94) *The Hearing Review, (Disability regulations review)*
Patricia M. Sullivan, PhD., Patrick E. Brookhouser, MD., John F.
        Knutson, PhD., John M. Scanlan, MD., Laura E. Schulte,
        PhD., (3-91) *Annals of Otology, Rhinology & Laryngology,*
        (Patterns of physical and sexual abuse of comm. hndcp. children)
Benna Timperlake, (1995) *The Endeavor (CA), (President's column)*
Abigail Trafford, (11-94) *The Washington Post (DC), (The brave new*
        world of genetic planning)
Charles Trueheart, (2-94) *LA Times-Washington Post Service, (Canadians*
        debate new restrictions on speech, press freedoms)
Graham H. Turner, (Winter-94) *Signpost, (Interview with Liisa Kaup-*
        pinen) Int'l Sign Linguistics Assoc., Univ. of Durham, England
Tom Willard, (11-94) *Silent News (NY), (A coming of age...)*
April Witt, (10-95) *Silent News (NY), (Arrest uncalled for...)*
Cathy Young, (11-93) *Philadelphia Inquirer (PA), (Some deaf won't join*
        the hearing)
Warren Wilson (12-95) *Seattle P-I (WA), (Computers learning to listen...)*

NO DIGNITY FOR JOSHUA

PERTINENT INFORMATION REGARDING THE NOTES SECTION:
The information in the notes section is provided as a source of further information for the reader and compliance with the U.S. Copyright laws regarding "fair use." The reader should not assume the positions on any subject matter of the source authors in the notes section without having read their actual writings. Those authors may, or may not, have been citing the positions of others, quoting others or simply engaged in a general discussion of the subject.

2-1	Males
2-2	Sullivan et al, LaBarre, Knutson-Sullivan
2-3	Knutson 96, LaBarre, Sullivan et al
2-4	Silent News 1-95, Kafka, AP 10-96, Bristol Herald-Courier 10-96
2-5	LaBarre
2-6	Deaf Life 7-93 ("leading concern"), Knutson-Sullivan ("discovery")
2-7	LeBarre, Sullivan et al
2-8	Deaf Life 4-93, 7-93
2-9	Parsons
2-10	Deaf Life 7-93 ("break this vicious cycle")
2-11	Ryther 10-96 *(Abuse: It happens every day)*
2-12	Bristol Herald-Courier 10-96 *(Panel suggests stricter oversight...)*
3-1	Golan 95, Golan 96, Solomon, Young
3-2	Menzel 2-94 *(Give me liberty or give me deaf?)*
3-3	Golan 95
3-4	De Mers
3-5	Solomon
3-6	Imada
3-7	Life After Deafness 10-94 ("backlash"), Saunders 9-95 *(State that has language law shows it's not enforceable)* ("preserve"), Parsons ("defiance")
3-8	Lovley (tba)-95 ("hang together"), McCullough-Menzel ("trivial differences"), Young ("hard-core multiculturism")
3-9	Saevig ("historical comparison"), Lovley 2-95, 9-95 ("bickering")
3-10	Powell
3-11	Ryther 11-95 *(Killer Pens)*
3-12	Lovley (tba)-95
3-13	Roth
3-14	NAD/FOLDA-USA Position on Deaf Terminologies 1996
3-15	USA Today/AP Wire Reports (1995) quoting Teresa Ezzell, an official at Gallaudet
3-16	Scoggins ("NAD")
3-17	Gose ("poor English"), Christiansen-Barnartt ("cultural diversity")
3-18	Deaf Life 7-93 ("deaf trashing"), Deaf Life 2-95 ("finally recognizing"), Willard 11-94 ("historic shift")
3-19	Deaf Life 12-94 *The ASL/SEE-II debate: Moving forward.*
3-20	Deaf Life 2-95 ("prominent leader" is Dr. Frank Turk), Moore ("he's the one"), Sonnenstrahl ("hospital")
3-21	Apperson, Silent News/AP-San Francisco 1-95 ("lawsuits"), Hammack ("all-deaf rape trial")

104

3-22   Parker ("sports radio"), NAD Broadcaster 7-95 ("ACLU"), Schulberg ("benefits of Closed Captioning")

4-1   AP Wire Reports 3-95 *Languages may end up on cultural ecosystem's endangered species list* ("rapidly declining")

4-2   Golan 95 & 96 ("outspoken author")

4-3   Golan 95

4-4   Balkany et al ("further segregate'), Timperlake ("wide variety")

4-5   Solomon (quoting MJ Bienvenu)

4-6   Parsons

4-7   Golan 96 ("legislation, leaving the profession")

4-8   Deaf Action Comm. for Sign Writing, 1994 LaJolla, CA

4-9   Golan 95 ("small percentage"), Colon ("bridge"), Parsons ("higher level of English")

4-10   Golan 95 ("proposing"), Filips (quoting Frank Jazowick), Golan 95 ("not possible"), Soderfeldt ("recent study")

4-11   Am. Annals of the Deaf 4-96

4-12   Beck ("turmoil"), AP Wire reports 2-96 ("immigrants")

4-13   Golan 96 ("basis for success"), Ryther 1-95 ("fabric"), Lependorf 10-93 quoting Tom Willard ("master both")

4-14   Elton

4-15   Am. Annals of the Deaf 4-93 ("evidence"), Ryther 1-95 ("publicly")

4-16   Robinette 2-93 ("$9,000/$44,000/$429,000"), NIH Consensus Statement 1992 ("$420 billion")

4-17   Solomon (quoting Oscar Cohen)

4-18   Parsons ("professors"), Oliver ("published reports")

4-19   Cohen 96

4-20   Caswell

4-21   Kramer

5-1   Christiansen-Barnartt ("new disclosures"), Deaf Life 12-94 ("mis-interpretations" and "two student leaders supported hearing candidate for president") Koppel ("anarchy")

5-2   Menzel 10-95 *Self-reliance* ("observation"), Firth 7-95 ("rise")

5-3   Silent News 10-95 ("common sense"), Strom ("deaf woman sues"), Lependorf 1-95 ("frivolous")

5-4   Saunders 2-96 ("downright unappeasable")

5-5   Crockett ("without merit"), Deaf Life 11-95 *(Deaf patient sues doctor under the ADA--And loses)* ("court decision")

5-6   Dixon ("SSI no longer an entitlement"), Rosenblatt ("reviewing") The Community Ear 12-95 ("obstacle")

5-7   Golan 96 ("academically undemanding"), Parsons ("no longer hire"), Golan 95 ("not our problem")

5-8   Calif. Dept. of Rehabilitation Survey 1993

5-9   Lew Golan's 3-96 article in The Washington Post

5-10   Colon

5-11   Silent News 1-95 ("shortages"), Solomon ("shortages"), Kleiman ("advocates," interviewing Janet Bailey)

5-12   Rogers

5-13   Trueheart ("Canadians")

5-14   Mack ("thought police")

5-15   Caswell ("evidence, expensive social club, abysmally"), Menzel 96 ("not deserving of the name")

5-16   Witt (reporting on the arrest of Robyn Brooks)

5-17   Solomon ("Nazis," quoting MJ Bienvenu), Coffey ("not qualified," referring to a statement made by Dr. Roz Rosen) Deaf Life 11-95 ("lobotomies," letter from Dr. Harlan Lane)
5-18   Deaf Life 5-96 (interview with Paul Kiel)
5-19   Christiansen-Barnartt
5-20   Silent News 2-95
5-21   Colon (referring to comments by MJ Bienvenu)
5-22   Berringer
5-23   Golan 96
5-24   Manning
6-1   Young
6-2   Biderman ("media attention"), Solomon ("final solution" quoting Paddy Ladd), Balkany et al ("confused and angry')
6-3   William House CI Study Group 1993 letters on file ("confusion about the CI), also ("no longer exist" quote from Prof. Barbara White at Gallaudet)
6-4   Berringer ("birthright of silence"), Silver ("Nazi experiments")
6-5   Turner ("unethical"), Andersson ("died," writer is president of the WFD) Balkany et al ("research results") Solomon ("complications are rare")
6-6   Balkany et al
6-7   Balkany et al, Solomon, Shamir (a sarcastic, but accurate look at a contradiction by culturally-deaf leaders)
6-8   Berlin
6-9   Am. Journal of Otology 11-94 ("major university," U. of Iowa and NYU School of Medicine), Assc. Press 5-95 ("NIH comments" updated figures from new source)
6-10   Biderman
6-11   CI Symposium, Miami, 1996
6-12   Biderman ("high costs"), Cohen 1994 ("lose money")
6-13   Menzel 96
6-14   Filips (quoting Tom Holcomb)
6-15   Menzel 2-94 *(Give me liberty or give me deaf?)*
6-16   Balkany et al
6-17   Caplan
6-18   Glausiusz ("usher's syndrome"), Trafford ("very close")
6-19   ABC Nightline 5-96 ("short stature"), Trafford ("pre-natal" "alternative style")
7-1   The Community Ear 8-96 report regarding the actor Jeremy Irons
7-2   Emerick ("deaf-phobia")
7-3   Merker ("medical profession")
7-4   Wilson ("voice recognition")

INDEX

Also available from Kodiak Media Group...

A CHILD SACRIFICED
TO THE DEAF CULTURE
By Tom Bertling

What others are saying about this book...

"...A masterpiece...gripping...powerful...the author's outstanding legacy to the world."
> -*Prof. Frances Parsons,*
> GALLAUDET UNIVERSITY

"...opened my eyes to a new perspective on cultural deafness...this information is vital to parents..."
> -*Dr. Thomas Balkany, M.D.,*
> *Professor of Otology,*
> UNIVERSITY OF MIAMI

"One hopes this book will be read by members of the deaf community with an eye towards critical self evaluation."
> -*Dr. Lloyd Lamb,*
> AMERICAN JOURNAL OF OTOLOGY

"Tom Bertling swims where few dare to tread..."
> -*Paula Bonillas, Publisher*
> HEARING HEALTH

"A remarkable new book...at first hand, the author explains the motives of the deaf leaders...should be required reading..."
> -*Otto J. Menzel, Ph.D., Editor*
> LIFE AFTER DEAFNESS

NO DIGNITY FOR JOSHUA

More about A CHILD SACRIFICED...

"...a heartfelt book, worthy of reading by anyone interested in hearing issues...you'll be amazed at the book."
> *-Shawn Lovley, Book Reviewer*
> *ALDA NEWS*

"...clear, concise, and to the point... easy reading, entertaining...brings 'forbidden topics' up for discussion..."
> *-Tom Bradford, Author*
> *SAY THAT AGAIN, PLEASE!*

"...we appreciated the honesty...One can hope that it would be a mirror for some in the deaf community..."
> *-Daniel White, Coordinator*
> *GOODRICH CENTER FOR THE DEAF*

"...(the author) achieves his goal in as unbiased manner as possible...It never ceased to stir heated, animated conversation (among colleagues having read the book)..."
> *-John Reade, Past Director*
> *ACEHI NEWSLETTER (CANADA)*

"...a **must read**...a lively, readable book...the writer pulls no punches..."
> *-Terry Ryther, Book Reviewer*
> *THE COMMUNITY EAR*

"...very well thought out, eloquently written...I had a great time reading the book..."
> *-Damian Brown, Reviewer*
> *DEAF USA* KTESTM6./C/96-

USE ORDER FORM ON THE NEXT PAGE

APR 1 6 1998

NO DIGNITY FOR JOSHUA

NO DIGNITY FOR JOSHUA

A CHILD SACRIFICED

Both by Tom Bertling

Order these books today!

QUANTITY	BOOK TITLE	PRICE EACH	TOTAL
	"No Dignity for Joshua"	$21.95	
	"A Child Sacrificed"	$21.95	
		Handling fee	+ $4.95
		TOTAL DUE	

MAKE CHECK OR MONEY ORDER PAYABLE TO:
KODIAK MEDIA GROUP
PO BOX 1029-J2
WILSONVILLE, OREGON 97070

1 BOOK FOR $21.95, (PLUS $4.95 HANDLING FEE) TOTAL $26.90
2 BOOKS FOR $43.90, MIX OR MATCH, (PLUS $4.95 HANDLING FEE) TOTAL $48.85
3 BOOKS FOR $65.85, MIX OR MATCH, (PLUS $4.95 HANDLING FEE) TOTAL $70.80
4 BOOKS FOR $87.80, MIX OR MATCH, (PLUS $4.95 HANDLING FEE) TOTAL $92.75
5 BOOKS FOR $109.75 OR 6 BOOKS FOR $131.70, HANDLING FEE WAIVED
RUSH ORDERS MAILED WITHIN 5 BUSINESS DAYS, ADD $2.95 PER BOOK.
CANADIAN ORDERS, CHECK OR MONEY ORDER IN U.S. DOLLARS.
FOREIGN ORDERS, CHECK OR M/O IN US DOLLARS DRAWN ON A U.S. BANK.

PLEASE PRINT CLEARLY!

NAME_____

ADDRESS_____

CITY_____

STATE_____ ZIP_____ PH.(____)_____